Lamb's Tales

LAMB'S TALES

Allan Lamb and Peter Smith

London
GEORGE ALLEN & UNWIN
Boston   Sydney

**George Allen & Unwin (Publishers) Ltd,
40 Museum Street, London WC1A 1LU, UK**

George Allen & Unwin (Publishers) Ltd,
Park Lane, Hemel Hempstead, Herts HP2 4TE, UK

Allen & Unwin Inc.,
Fifty Cross Street, Winchester, Mass 01890, USA

George Allen & Unwin Ltd,
8 Napier Street, North Sydney, NSW 2060, Australia

First published in 1985

0 04 796101 5

Set in 11 on 13 point Palatino by Nene Phototypesetters, Northampton
and printed in Great Britain by Butler & Tanner Ltd, Frome and London

Contents

To: My Mum and Dad

Illustrations

Photographer: Adrian Murrell/All Sport

Illustrations

CHAPTER 1

Hardly an Indian Summer

There has never been a tour like the England one to India at the end of 1984. I fervently hope there will never be another ever to compare with it either from a cricketing viewpoint or from the suffering we witnessed by the people of India to the people of India.

There was the assassination of India's Prime Minister Mrs Indira Gandhi within five hours of our arrival in the country to launch the tour, an act which threw the whole country into turmoil especially in Delhi where the shooting had taken place little more than a five minute walk away from our hotel. We were caught up in the bloody aftermath as Hindu turned upon Sikh in extracting horrific revenge, two of Mrs Gandhi's Sikh bodyguards having turned on her with a pistol and a sub machine gun as she walked from her residence to her office where she was going to give a filmed interview to playwright and actor Peter Ustinov who was waiting nearby.

That one act was horrifying enough, wrecking the whole tour schedule as the country was plunged into official mourning during which any form of entertainment was banned, many a large area close to a complete breakdown of law and order as whole Sikh communities were slaughtered, Sikh owned businesses set on fire. As always in such situations, there were others who used the tragedy for their own personal gain by looting, making the task of securing the towns even harder for the police and troops.

I thought we would be back in England by the first weekend. The newspaper stories of arson, looting, mass slaughter painted such an alarming picture, there seemed no possible way the tour could go ahead as the first three matches were scrubbed, others

1

placed in doubt. We were all advised by the British High Commission in Delhi not to set foot outside the doors of the Taj Palace Hotel where we were staying, a luxury hotel in the upper class residential belt of New Delhi favoured by High Commission staff and embassy staff of other countries. An attractive area with broad, tree lined avenues.

If that advice had not been forthcoming from the High Commission we could not have gone out in the evenings if we had wanted to with a curfew in force from dusk to dawn, the army patrolling the streets in trucks equipped with sten and sub machine guns with shoot on sight orders.

We ventured out only twice in our five day stay. Once for a practice session in the British High Commission compound. Another time to join the staff for a drink at their club. The rest of the time was spent in the hotel, trying to keep our minds on cricket, the need to remain fit by using the hotel gymnasium where I ran five miles every morning on a machine. Most of the lads did the same.

Although we were involved in the whole tragic mess because we were stopped from playing cricket, it was a mess from which we could remain detached to a large extent. But the violence still hit us. Hit us hard having taken place only three weeks after the IRA attempt to assassinate Mrs Margaret Thatcher and other Government ministers with the bomb in the Grand Hotel, Brighton.

It hit us because we see and even taste the extent of the violence. From the hotel swimming pool it was possible to see over an immaculately trimmed hedge, the truck loads of troops being ferried in helping to restore calm around Mrs Gandhi's residence, the hospital where her bullet riddled body was taken and the hall where she was lying in state. Still more rushing to the old city of Delhi.

From our hotel rooms up on the ninth floor we had a panoramic view looking across towards Old Delhi and could see parts of it going up in smoke. A resident of Delhi helped to identify the trouble regions. One thick black plume of smoke was a Sikh owned oil storage depot which kept burning throughout the day after Mrs Gandhi's death. Another was a Sikh owned hotel. A third a school for Sikh children. Yet others – sometimes with flames leaping towards the sky – more business premises of Sikh owners. Here and there smaller fires as taxis owned or driven by Sikhs were stopped and set alight.

We saw it at closer hand too as the hotel rapidly filled up with television crews from all around the world swarming in to cover Mrs Gandhi's funeral and cremation. Rooms taken, too, by refugees from the violence, one English family fleeing from their Sikh owned hotel in Old Delhi with only the clothes in which they were dressed after their hotel had been stormed and set on fire.

I must admit I was apprehensive. And I was not alone. Several of us were a little concerned about the length of time it seemed to be taking to reach a decision about our immediate future and a lack of information about what was going to happen or even might happen to us all. It was not until later that we started to appreciate the problems confronting our manager Tony Brown, the Somerset secretary and former Gloucestershire medium paced bowler who was making his first visit to the country.

He knew exactly what he wanted but was not at complete liberty to tell us everything because of the diplomatic channnels he was forced to go through and the difficulty he had in contacting Indian Board officials and even Lord's because the assassination had strained the communication services. He proved a winner in getting us out to Sri Lanka five days after we had landed in India although the Indian Board officials were reluctant, at first, to let us go.

It was essential we went. Both for our own peace of mind and to be able to play cricket. There is nothing worse for a cricketer than being forced to sit around and do nothing when all he wants to do is go out and play. A day spent at a county ground in England when rain has washed out play is a day to forget. In Delhi we had five days virtually doing nothing – and plenty of time to think.

Sri Lanka was a master stroke. A chance to practise. A chance to play a game. A chance to relax, walk around freely, taste food in other restaurants instead of being cooped up in the hotel coffee shop. Yet Colombo also seemed full of troops, on the alert for a Tamil uprising that was to break out just after we left. Two days after our departure, Colombo was placed under a 48 hour curfew. We got out in time.

Strangely I was more apprehensive in Delhi than I was in Bombay a month later when we were hit by a second tragedy – and one much nearer home. That was the murder of Percy Norris, the

3

Deputy British High Commissioner in Bombay just 24 hours before the first Test was due to start and only a few hours after we had left his company at a party he had thrown in our honour in his flat. That was a death, a wicked murder, we could stretch out our hands and feel. It shocked us all.

It shocked some of us even more deeply than I realised at the time for it was not until after we had played that first Test and lost that I discovered how nervous some of the players had felt when they walked out into the Wankhede Stadium on the first day.

For a moment after that murder we again thought we would be flying home. If the decision about going or staying had been left to the players, there is no doubt that all would have opted to go within the first hour of hearing of the latest tragedy to hit the tour. Yet, within a matter of hours, the opinion and mood had changed dramatically. By that evening on the eve of the Test I believe all of the team were willing to stay and do the job we had come to do.

That was another success for Tony Brown, his quiet persuasive way and the manner in which he conducted himself, smoothing fears, outwardly calm and in control whatever his inner feelings might have been.

Mr Norris' murder touched us more than Mrs Gandhi's assassination because he was English. There was the additional speculation that the timing had been chosen deliberately because we were in the city and the Test match was about to start. The suggestion that we, too, could be involved. Above all was the fact that we had all spent such a great time in their company the evening before.

He was a genial, affable host, our visit one of his first engagements having taken up office only a few weeks before. He was a cricket fan. He was pleased to see us, kept telling us how much he was looking forward to coming to the matches. Along with his charming wife Angela, he was waiting at the door to greet us, their natural friendliness making us feel welcome the moment we stepped over the doorway. The rest of the company was good, too. Other members of the High Commission staff in Bombay, a few businessmen and a few representatives from other High Commissions. After all our troubles of the previous four weeks, everything seemed to be fitting into place. We were all geared up for the Test, sorry when we had to leave their company but an early departure essential for the last net session planned for 9.30 the following morning.

First there was a photographic session the following morning on the lawns of the Taj Mahal Hotel which overlooks the main harbour of Bombay, the gateway to India and the Arabian Sea. The photograph of the team which traditionally adorns the Christmas Cards we send home from every tour. A happy session but one to be spoilt within minutes as Tony Brown asked us to report to the team room.

He had been telephoned by then and informed of Mr Norris' murder which had taken place only 70 minutes before. He knew when the photographs were being taken but disguised his feelings. Norman Gifford, our assistant manager, also knew. So did David Gower and physiotherapist Bernard Thomas. So did off-spinner Pat Pocock who had met the Norris family a year earlier in Dubai along with his wife Diane and become firm friends. He had phoned the Norris family home early that morning to say thank you for the previous evening and pass on a message from his wife only to be told that Mr Norris had been murdered just a few minutes earlier. Pat was one of the first in the world to learn of the tragedy.

The rest of us were told by the manager. We were informed that the net practice had been cancelled and that we were to stay in the hotel until further arrangements had been made and the position had become clear.

After all that had happened to us since we left England exactly one month before, we thought that was the end. We couldn't see the tour going ahead now. There was one, possibly two murderers at loose in Bombay who has carefully selected a British subject as their target. It was obviously a professional job that had been carried out after weeks of planning. But was it pure coincidence that we were also in Bombay? That thought was in our minds as rumours spread throughout the hotel of British businesses being boarded up and closed, warnings issued to British residents in Bombay to stay indoors and not move around.

It was against this background that we were suddenly informed by David Gower and Mike Gatting that we were to practise after all, news that brought a response from some of 'do you mean net practice or target practice?' It was said as a joke but it also showed the feeling of apprehension and tension inside the party.

5

1   Allan Lamb at net practice before the 2nd Test at Delhi in December 1984.

None of us were looking forward to going to the Wankhede Stadium. I imagine we would all have felt even worse if we had known that the coach taking us to the ground passed the actual spot where Mr Norris had been gunned down in his white official Rover car only four hours before. Fortunately nobody pointed it out to us. We passed that very spot every day afterwards going to and from the ground for the Test match. I learned the shooting had taken place on one of the busy crossroads we went through but never identified the actual one and I don't think any of the lads ever found out.

As it turned out, the decision to go ahead with the net session was the saving of the party, the best move the tour management could have made. We were nervous about entering the stadium. Nervous about walking out in the huge, concrete bowl that can hold 50,000 spectators. Nervous about the men who were walking around the rooftop putting the finishing touches to the two scoreboards, hanging advertising posters. Nervous about others on the rooftops of buildings overlooking the ground. Two or three players told me afterwards they could not help glancing up and wondering whether any one of those tiny figures might be a sniper. It was a natural reaction.

The net started slowly. Our minds elsewhere. Yet, within half an hour, the professionalism of all the players came through. Once they found a bat or ball in hand, the cricketer emerged. It was a good net, the mood of the whole party rapidly changing. As Tony Brown was to say afterwards, the actual playing of the game concentrated the mind on cricket, eliminating most other thoughts. There was a suggestion that the start should be delayed 24 hours but that was rejected by the tour management. I believe it was a right decision. If the tour was not to be abandoned, the sooner we were involved in cricket the better.

The net session was followed by another team meeting when it was explained the match would go ahead as planned, assurances having been received from every possible authority that we were not at risk. That made us feel better especially when we returned to our rooms and found armed police stationed outside every door. That is something we have got used to on tour now.

The mood of the whole party was changing rapidly now. We were all more relaxed, perhaps the turning point was the knowlege that Mrs Norris had taken the trouble to phone Tony Brown and ask that the match should go ahead as planned because her husband would have wanted it that way. She even took the trouble the following morning along with her daughter Madeline of sending another message wishing us luck. It was a nice, human touch.

Luck was one commodity we had been without on the tour. We had not got as much out of our week in Sri Lanka as we had hoped because an out of season monsoon storm had wrecked the most important game, a one day match billed as a full international by the locals, when we came across 10 of the 11 players who had embarrassed us in the Test match at Lord's only six weeks earlier. At 178 for five looking good for a possible 220 plus from their 45 overs when the heavens opened, it would have provided us with a stiff examination. It was cruel luck on them after their authorities had done so much in such a short time to take us in. Within half an hour the entire ground was flooded. As was our dressing room.

The rain was so intense it was impossible for us to get to our coach without getting saturated. But we were getting saturated from the inside too as water gushed down the steps of the dressing room and formed a lake over the tiled floor. Kit had to be dumped on tables whilst we sat around marooned on chairs waiting for the rain to ease, the foot deep torrent of water on the roads outside to subside.

In Ahmedamad on the second match of the Indian tour we had betrayed our talent against the India Under-25 when losing by an innings and 59 runs. Our approach was wrong, too carefree and abandoned. But the defeat had served as a warning, a lesson to us all. It was disappointing to lose but it opened our eyes – both the newcomers to touring and the older hands in the side – to the ways of cricketing life in India which are not always in accord with what we have been used to at home or, indeed, in other parts of the world.

That lesson went home as was shown by an entirely different approach in Rajkot against the West Zone team. Admittedly the wicket was so slow a timeless test played there would go on forever. It was difficult to get out as Mike Gatting demonstrated when he tried to after scoring his century in order to give others a chance to bat. But the approach had been right, care and attention paid to every detail in the innings. The loose strokes restricted to a bare minimum.

We had felt happy, even a little confident when we returned to Bombay to prepare for that first Test. The mood was right. Everybody had made runs among the first six batsmen at some stage or another. Perhaps wickets had been a little hard to come by on the Indian tracks but Norman Cowans was showing a fair turn of pace and better control than on previous tours. Phil Edmonds had bowled some superb spells despite having a mental block about where he should put his feet during his run up. Pat Pocock's infectious enthusiasm had spread among the 16 party. He was bowling well, too.

Yet we also knew we would need a little luck on our side to come through the first Test ordeal on a wicket which promised a result playing an Indian side back under the direction of Sunny Gavaskar and seeking to end a 31 Test match run without a victory. Without a victory, in fact, since beating England on the same Bombay wicket at the start of Keith Fletcher's 1981–82 tour.

With the wicket looking as if it would help the spinners sometime early on the fourth day onwards, winning the toss was essential and David did his job there. But that was about all that went right for us on the first day – the day the Test was really lost.

David said later that something in the region of 250 for three at the close of the first day should have been par in the conditions facing an Indian attack that was neat, tidy but not menacing. Instead we finished it at 190 for nine, our chance blown despite Graeme Fowler and Tim Robinson – making his Test debut along with Chris Cowdrey – putting on 46 runs without too much concern before they were parted.

Critics with far greater touring experience than I or any other member of the team, have since told me that they linked our first day performance with the death of Mr Norris and the events over the previous 24 hours. Maybe they are right although I never once linked the events at the time. My mind was perfectly clear. The Test match was on, I was keyed up for it. I was thinking about nothing else but batting when I walked to the wicket with the score on 78 for three. I was certainly not worried about my safety. The thought that I could be in any danger had never entered my head. Neither do I attribute my downfall to any other reason than the ball stopping a little as I attempted to whip a leg stump half volley from Kapil Dev through midwicket only to give a catch to mid-on when I had made only nine.

2   Laxman Sivaramakrishnan, the 18 year old leg spinner who took 12–181 in the first Test in Bombay.

Looking back perhaps we kidded ourselves our minds were fully pre-occupied with the actual playing of the game. Perhaps just a little part was not concentrating fully to explain the succession of strokes which brought about our first day downfall. It wasn't the umpiring. It wasn't only the ability of 18-year-old leg spinner Laxman Sivaramakrishnan playing his first Test match in his own country after going wicketless on his Test debut in the West Indies 18 months previously when he had become the youngest player to appear for India.

He is a good bowler. Not good enough, in my opinion, to have finished that first innings with six for 64 and finished the match with 12 for 181.

Sivaramakrishnan certainly had good fortune on his side throughout which, I suppose, is only appropriate for his complete name is made up of the names of four gods strung together. He had every encouragement to settle down quickly, his fourth ball claiming the wicket of Graeme Fowler, a full toss which Graeme hit straight back.

He was distraught at getting out in such a way but the quality of Graeme is his ability to put disasters immediately behind him and come bouncing back. He could even see a humorous side in the end having been bowled by a full toss in his previous innings in Rajkot. 'At least I'm getting better at playing them now because I managed to get a bat on this one,' he said.

That was the start of Sivaramakrishnan's hold which was broken only by the ever reliable Paul Downton and Phil Edmonds during a 61 stand in our first innings and by Graeme Fowler, Mike Gatting and Downton again in our second innings.

Yet it was pleasing to be in a dressing room that remained free of any complex about the leg spinner. He is a good bowler but not in the class of Pakistan's Abdul Qadir. At 18 he is still learning his trade and does not possess Qadir's control or variation. What he does possess is Qadir's aggressive approach, never afraid to lodge an appeal which worked in his favour more than once. Quick to show a flash of anger too when an appeal is turned down.

Even though he got me out in the second innings when I was stumped, I have no qualms about facing him. David Gower and Mike Gatting felt the same way and the others in the side felt comfortable if a little more unsure.

If our first innings approach had been a little out of character, so

11

3   Swarup Kishen, controversial Indian umpire 1st Test in Bombay.

had that of the Indian side when they batted in their first innings, going off with a rush that was astonishing. It was almost a shot a ball with 120 of their first 156 runs coming in boundaries as if they were using up all their nervous energy at once. Nervous they were too against the bowling of Norman Cowans who had them jumping with his pace and bounce once he had warmed up.

He made two quick strikes in dismissing Gavaskar – flashing at deliveries in a way I never expected to see from a man who is regarded as the grand master among opening batsmen – and Dilip Vengsarkar who had taken 200 off us in Rajkot. With Ashuman Gaekward being run out, Pat Pocock dismissing Mohinder Amarnath and Phil Edmonds accounting for Sandeep Patil, India had lost their first five for 156.

Another strike then and we would have been back in it but Ravi Shastri took over along with Kapil Dev to steady India and show the value of having two genuine all rounders batting six and seven in the order. When Dev went, in stepped Syed Kirmani to join Shastri in a record breaking seventh wicket partnership of 235 which put the game out of our reach. Each scored a century, Shastri's fourth in Test cricket, Kirmani's second. Only once did we have a real chance of separating them when Paul Downton missed a stumping chance against Shastri off Phil Edmonds when the batsman had made only 38 towards his eventual 142. Paul is a genuine enough guy not to make any excuses but we all felt sorry for him because he has fitted in so well since taking over from Bob Taylor.

In our second innings he again showed the strength he has brought to our lower order batting with a Test best score of 62. But that innings belonged almost exclusively to Mike Gatting in scoring his first Test century at his 54th attempt. It was a remarkably long time coming for a player with such commanding ability, who absolutely murders attacks just below the very best. There was a tear in his eye when he cover drove Sivaramakrishnan for four, relief in the hearts of the rest of us as we stood to applaud our vice captain. He had overcome the hurdle at last. The horizon was now clear. There would be more to come as Bobby Simpson, the former Australian captain, had demonstrated when he had to wait until his 30th Test before scoring his first century at Old Trafford in 1964. We couldn't help pointing out to Mike that Simpson had gone on to score 311 on that occasion.

4   Mike Gatting on his way to his third consecutive century in the One Day
International at Pune in December 1984.

At least Mike's 138 coupled with an innings of 55 from Graeme Fowler plus Paul Downton's contribution and another innings of 22 from Pat Pocock enabled us to avoid the indignity of an innings defeat. But India were left with only 48 to get to complete a victory that had looked booked for them from the moment Shastri and Kirmani had shared their partnership.

After such a traumatic start to the tour, it would not have been surprising if a few heads had started to drop following the first Test defeat especially as we remained convinced that not all the second innings dismissals had been genuine. Instead the opposite was true. The team spirit was superb, remarkably so considering that there were 10 newcomers to India in the party, four players who had never played for England before the tour started. But the mix was superb, a tour of India throwing the players together in a united bunch. The spirit was a triumph for the management team. The desire to win the first one day international in Pune two days later was astonishing.

Once again we had Mike Gatting to thank. Four days after scoring his first Test century for his country, he scored his first one day century for England in masterminding our effort to overhaul India's 214 for six built around a century by Vengsarkar.

We had looked in trouble at 47 for three, the third wicket being mine when I changed my mind about hitting Manoj Prabhakar's slower ball over the top and gave him a simple return catch instead. We looked in even deeper trouble when we were 129 for six, that total boosted by a 67 run partnership in 14 overs by Mike and Vic Marks – promoted up the order with our captain still suffering from a bleeding nose after being hit whilst in the field.

That was when Mike showed his class along with the company of Paul Downton, their years of success in one day cricket at home with Middlesex enabling them to overcome the crisis in the most sensible way.

In Mike's eventual unbeaten 115 in our four wicket victory, no less than 44 had come in singles, a high proportion for a man who normally scores in boundaries. He worked the field superbly to keep the score moving at the five an over rate we wanted when Paul joined him and there was never any danger.

It was a fact some in the crowd recognised before the end, announcing the defeat before it had been achieved when they took out their anger on the Indian side by hurling bottles on to the outfield, causing a 17 minute hold-up when we wanted just seven to win with 20 balls remaining.

For a moment it looked ugly as the fielders plus Mike and Paul were forced to huddle in the middle whilst order was restored. Yet another incident on the tour. This time we did not mind. It meant we were on top. Victory was ours. The tour was starting from that moment.

We felt settled at last. For even between the assassination of Mrs Gandhi and the murder of Mr Norris we had felt ill at ease with the schedule seemingly changing every other day. When we arrived in one centre, we were never really sure where we would be going next. In addition the misfortunes of Martyn Moxon had touched us all, such a close knit party that what hurt one, hurt the rest of us.

Back in England he had been denied the chance of his Test debut when forced to pull out of the Lord's game against the West Indies two days after his selection because of a cracked rib injury – received playing against Northants. Before he had a chance to be selected for a match in Sri Lanka, he had fallen victim to a flu and stomach bug which left him weak and pale.

Then, worst of all, the tragic news on our last evening in Colombo that his father had been taken seriously ill, forcing Martyn to fly home only to be told on his arrival at Gatwick Airport his father had died. That affected us all because we knew that Martyn was an only child and that his father, a keen cricket administrator and coach during his younger days, had so looked forward to seeing his son play for his country. By the time Martyn was free to return, it was too late to be in contention for the first Test. He bore it all with tremendous courage, even the leg pull by the rest of the lads who nicknamed him criss cross because he had spent so much time in the nets under the burning Indian sun it had left a sunburned criss cross pattern on his exposed skin.

If my experiences of playing against India had produced the extremes in emotions it is fitting for India itself is a country of extremes. In Jaipur the tour management produced a master stroke in removing us from a hotel where it was impossible to get hot water and where the air conditioning either did not work or kept one awake and switched us to the magnificent Rambagh Palace. It was a dream.

My own room shared with Tim Robinson occupied two floors. The bedroom on one level and then stairs leading up to a dining area on another. Tony Brown's room was so large he was able to get his full length run in between the walls while David Gower was awarded the 'Princess Suite' no doubt as a result of those blonde curls of his. Again his suite was so large he felt it posed problems for him. Having to make sudden dashes to the bathroom is part and parcel of touring India, an occupational hazard that can strike at any time of the day or night – and did frequently. David was worried that when it struck him, the bathroom was so far away he would not make it in time.

The whole place was sensational, a true palace built among immaculately mowed lawns on which peacocks strutted proudly. A place that had to be seen to be believed. So had our hotel two matches on in Rajkot although for entirely the opposite reason.

Not even a bath there. Just four concrete walls serving as a bathroom which contained a sink which sometimes provided hot water, another tap and two buckets as the shower arrangement. And the mosquitoes by the thousands just waiting to swoop on the innocent victims. Filling the rooms at night, flying in swarms above our heads in the hastily arranged dining room, the hotel being a vegetarian establishment. If ever there was a hotel designed to test team spirit, that was the one. Fortunately, the team spirit conquered all.

In between there was Ahmedabad. An industrial town swarming with people in the dry state of Gujarat where visitors like ourselves needed to obtain special licences in order to buy a bottle of beer. Except the beer was so bad we never bothered.

We played against India's Under-25 team in the town's latest pride and joy, a new Test stadium that was built within eight months, cost £1½ million pounds and houses 55,000 people at present, soon to hold 85,000 when fully completed to make it the third largest Test playing ground in the world.

Yet, in getting there from our hotel in the middle of the town to the new stadium on the edge of the town, we had to pass some of the worst slums I have ever seen in my life – far worse living conditions than exist in the townships in South Africa which have been condemned by black nations throughout the world as horrific.

In Ahmedabad there were mudhuts on the dried out river banks seemingly built on top of each other. Wooden shacks no more than eight foot wide and deep housing whole families, built so crazily and precariously it appeared that if one collapsed it would have a domino effect and the rest would fall down. People living in canvas shelters on the roadside, any odd piece of waste ground. Begging, scrapping, pleading for a living and food.

Driving past such places each day was a chastening experience too. Here we were worried about our own safety, concerned with our own problems, wondering whether the tour was going ahead, cricket was going to be played yet a glance out of the window made us realise our troubles were nothing compared to the problems of those outside our coach. And sad, too.

I had no such inkling, of course, what life in India was all about back in 1982 when I was first chosen for England. But I did have worries then especially when my name was being touted in the newspapers for an England call-up long before the first squad was due to be announced.

In a way I probably have the late Mrs Indira Gandhi to thank for the opportunity for it was her personal decision to allow England's 1981/82 tour of India to go ahead when several government ministers, anti-apartheid groups and student organisations demanded the tour should be cancelled because England's party contained Geoff Boycott and my Northants' colleague Geoff Cook who had both played cricket in South Africa.

If the tour had been called off because of their presence there was no way India would have agreed to play against me in 1982 but for their Prime Minister's approval.

Whether the Test and County Cricket Board had spoken with their opposite numbers from the Indian Board and mentioned the possibility of me being chosen for England to see if there was any objection, I shall never know. But I was concerned about possible reaction even when I first heard that I was in the 13 England named for the opening one day international at Headingley.

As I have already mentioned my selection caused more headlines than it would otherwise have done for it was the first match England played without the services of those players who had joined in the 'rebel' tour of South Africa only six weeks earlier. Another reason why I waited and wondered for the first two days after I had been chosen, thinking my world might explode. Thankfully, nothing happened.

I had very little to do with England's first victory at Headingley. Batting first India had been dismissed for 193, a target Barry Wood and Chris Tavare made look ridiculously easy. It was virtually all over when I walked to the wicket on Tav's dismissal and kept Barry company for a few minutes whilst he administered the final winning blow.

The next game at the Oval was different. This time we batted first and I soon found myself at the crease. Something of a hero even when making 99 of England's 276, getting out late in the innings trying to push the score along even faster when aiming for a boundary when a simple push would have been enough to earn a century. I discovered, too, the joy of batting with David Gower who made 76 in that innings, playing with such ease I envied his class and coolness. And have wished so many times since that we could have shared greater partnerships than we have done.

Still I was happy enough with 99. Happier still when I returned to the Oval five weeks later and scored my first Test century for England. I had made only nine followed by an unbeaten 37 on my Test debut when England won the first Test at Lord's. I made only nine in the one innings I played in the second Test at Old Trafford. I felt I needed a score at the Oval if I was going to retain my England place for the second half of the summer against Pakistan.

The platform was right with Geoff Cook and Chris Tavare putting on 96 for the first wicket. I was grateful, too, for the later help of Ian Botham who took all the pressure off me by wading into the Indian attack to the tune of 208 runs. I sat back, content with ones and twos, perhaps an occasional four during our 176 partnership together for the fourth wicket which was completely dominated by Ian smashing the ball to all parts.

He helped me, encouraged me, talked to me and eased me through to my century while he enjoyed himself at the other end, the grin growing broader by the minute under that floppy sun hat of his while his bat whirled away, stunning the Indian fielders and the crowd alike by the sheer speed with which he sent the ball to the boundary.

I was so overjoyed at having proved my worth I didn't even mind too strongly about the mix-up which resulted in me being stranded by yards and run out. I had 107 against my name which was followed by an unbeaten 45 in England's second innings of a drawn match.

It was the last match of the three match series, a series ending in a 1–0 victory for England avenging the 1–0 defeat in India only a few months before. I finished that game very thankful – and looking forward to the next Test series against India – little knowing of the pain, heartbreak and suffering that was to accompany that series in the winter of 1984/85.

CHAPTER 2

A bundle of suspicion despite four centuries

Colin Cowdrey was born in Ottacamund in the south of India of English parents. He would undoubtedly have been feted and headlined a national hero if he had still been playing in the summer of 1984 and had taken centuries off the West Indies in three successive Tests.

That would have been right and proper. They were, in the view of many cricketing experts whose opinions have been accepted as gospel, the best side the game has ever produced.

The same would have applied if Ted Dexter had been born some 20 years later than he was, enabling him to walk out at Lord's in the June of that same summer to produce an innings of 110 against Clive Lloyd's latest all conquering team and to follow it with an innings of 100 at Headingley plus an unbeaten 100 at Old Trafford.

That would have been no more than he would have deserved either, having been acclaimed a hero for doing far less during his 62 match Test career. Ted was born in Milan, Italy, of English parents.

I actually managed to do all that in the summer of '84 when getting the better of Malcolm Marshall, Joel Garner, Michael Holding and Eldine Baptiste, not forgetting Winston Davis. For an encore, I was the only England batsman to take a century off Sri Lanka when they came to Lord's at the end of the season, although the country seemed to expect the first four or five in the batting order to do the same.

You have got to go back to Denis Compton – another heroic

5   Allan Lamb scores his second century against the West Indies at Lord's during the second Test in 1984.

cricketing figure – in 1947 to find the last time an English summer was decorated by four Test centuries by an individual batsman from the home side.

Yet the praise I received was strangely muted, the headlines, in the main, offensive and critical. My situation was not eased by the fact none of the above brought about a victory. I arrived in this world in Langebaanweg of English born parents.

Langebaanweg? That is in South Africa. It made all the difference. And it hurt – deeply. For I gave blood, sweat and tears in making those runs in trying to save the cricketing reputation of a country I regard as home.

Unfortunately, after an unbroken run of 27 Test matches for England by the end of the 1984 summer, I may regard it as home but the vast majority of the people I represent still look upon me as a suspect, 5ft 8in, bundle of trouble. Someone who has little right to be sandwiched in the middle order between the elegant frame of David Gower, the country's captain, and the more robust one of Ian Botham.

I was still the interloper, the South African who had sneaked into the England side before the Test and County Cricket Board had time to close the door in their qualification laws just because the gateway into the Test arena I would normally have taken had been closed to me as a result of the world's abhorrence of the apartheid system in the country of my birth.

Yet I regard myself as just as English as Cowdrey or Dexter, despite the clipped accent that betrays my upbringing. As proud to play and fight for England against the most fearsome attack cricket has known as Compton was throughout his marvellous 78 Test match career which turned him into the game's first modern style super-star.

It is not my fault that the parents of Cowdrey and Dexter – or the many others born overseas but accepted into the England side without a murmur or suspicious glance – were temporary absentees from this country whereas mine were settled in South Africa and had made the country their home after being taken out there as youngsters by their respective parents.

That is the only difference between us, for which I was quite prepared to serve a four year qualifying period. Indeed, a period I thought I should endure. But it is a difference many others interpret as a great large, yawning gap which has meant years of

6 Allan Lamb moves his bat away – a rare movement for him – in the third Test at Headingley on his way to another century.

7 The West Indians can hardly restrain themselves at the capture of Lamb's wicket during the fourth Test at the Oval in August, 1984.

non recognition for me in many ways. Years that are far from over either.

I cannot help thinking how better off Zola Budd might be today if she had been made to serve a qualification period before being rushed into the United Kingdom team for the Los Angeles Olympic Games. It all appears to have been far too bewildering for a 17-year-old as she was at the time. It may even have ruined the great talent she undoubtedly possesses.

I don't blame Zola. Like myself, she wanted the opportunity to test herself against the best in the world and she was able to get that opportunity because of her English background. I do feel, however, the people responsible for bringing her over from South Africa and pushing her ahead should have had second thoughts before going ahead with their plans.

There was no need to have rushed her. Zola was way off her peak as a runner, the 1988 Olympic Games would have suited her better. If there had been a more strict qualification rule like the one I had to serve, Zola could have first discovered whether she was able to settle in England before committing herself to the country.

She could have eased herself into the way of life, made friends, found happiness before concentrating solely on her athletic prowess with the aim of striking for gold in 1988. Instead she found controversy, met opposition, hostility even, which could not have helped her prepare for Los Angeles especially as she was almost forced to lead the life of a recluse.

The whole scene has not done her any good and it has to be hoped it has not soured her so that she is lost to international athletics – and Great Britain – for good. And it will certainly not help the cause of others with English parentage but South African birth to be accepted in the future, especially if she does not return to England.

There is a constant reminder of my background and birthplace in reports of almost everything I do which sets me as a man apart and serves to feed further the minds of those who refuse to accept that I have a common link with almost everybody else in the England side – English born parents.

My lovely wife Lindsay who has sacrificed so much to support my career, faithfully keeps scrapbooks of almost everything written about me, particularly where Test matches are concerned.

And almost every Test match report contains the words 'South Africa' whenever they get around to my name.

If my contribution has been the main ingredient of the day, somewhere near the top of the story will be the words 'South African born Allan Lamb . . .' or 'Allan Lamb, the chunky South African born batsman . . .' or 'England's batsman from South Africa Allan Lamb . . .'

Always a label, always a tag. Never – or very seldom, just plain Allan Lamb full stop. Yet, in glancing through cricket books or actual match reports during the Cowdrey and Dexter years, I never found they were presented in a similar way.

Record books and biographies plus feature articles record somewhere that Cowdrey was born in India and that Dexter's birthplace was in Italy. But match reports never started 'Indian born Colin Cowdrey . . .' or 'Italian born Ted Dexter . . .'

I am not picking on these two much loved characters of English cricket or suggesting they had no right to be playing for England without any fuss being made about their presence. I am just using them to emphasise my point.

Instead I could easily have used the instance of G. O. 'Gubby' Allen, another former England captain and still one of the most respected figures in the game today. He was actually born in Australia. Or I could have used Bob Woolmer of Kent and England who was born in Kanpur, India, Derek Pringle of Essex and England who was born in Nairobi or Phil Edmonds whose birthplace was Lusaka, which is now Zambia, before coming to England to go to Cambridge University and then joining Middlesex.

In recent years, of course, England have picked two players who do not possess English-born parents in Roland Butcher and Norman Cowans who were born in Barbados and Jamaica respectively.

Both were raised in England and have every right to represent the country. Certainly I have no objection but I have always had the feeling that they were more readily accepted by the British public than I have been.

They have suffered the insults of a few mindless idiot hooligans who litter the odd county ground shouting obscenities under the influence of drink and through the safety of being in a crowd.

I was not alone in the Northants' side in feeling absolute disgust at Lord's during the NatWest semi-final against Middlesex in 1984 when a few beer swilling youngsters from Northamptonshire occupied the area in front of the Tavern Bar and taunted Norman Cowans when he was fielding a few yards in front of them on the third man boundary. They were not Northamptonshire supporters. The county can do without their kind.

'Butch' and 'Flash' Cowans suffered because of the colour of their skin, something that has never bothered me having played all my senior cricket whether at club level in South Africa or at a county and Test level in England in sides that have included both black and white players.

That, to the best of my knowledge, has been their only suffering as obnoxious as that is. I do not think they have suffered the resentment I have found in being South African born yet playing for England.

To be fair, I have not found any South African bias when playing for Northants. The people at the club and the supporters have treated me as though I were a Northamptonshire born and bred lad who came up through the local leagues.

They have appeared as proud of my performances for the county as they have been of the efforts of Wayne Larkins, Richard Williams, Geoff Cook and others in the side.

It is only when it comes to an international level that the feeling creeps inside me that I must do twice as well as anybody else in the England team if I am going to get any acknowledgement from outside, the public at large.

The difference was brought home to me with great force on the day after I had scored my third century against the West Indies when making that unbeaten 100 in the first innings at Old Trafford.

That evening I was having a drink with my wife and friends in the Cornhill reception area where the Test match sponsors make every player welcome following the end of a day's play. For a time I found myself in the company of two of the senior cricket writers who did congratulate me on my innings but one, a former England player, went on to say 'Wouldn't it be nice if an Englishman could do the same for England in the second innings.' Little wonder that I'm still left with a feeling that people consider me an outsider.

Perhaps I'm a little too sensitive on the subject. Yet it is difficult not to be when I still see letters in newspapers or cricket monthly magazines from people questioning my right to be playing for England.

Perhaps, too, it might have been different but for the unfortunate controversy splitting the game at the time I was being selected for England for the first time in the one day international series against India early in the 1982 summer.

Feeling was still running high about the three year ban from playing Test cricket imposed on Graham Gooch, John Emburey, Geoff Boycott and others for making up an English XI to go to South Africa in March that year to play a series of 'Test' and one day internationals.

At the time of my first selection for England, it was still not clear whether the so called 'rebels' were going to proceed with a threatened High Court action challenging the legality of the ban imposed by the Test and County Cricket Board. They were still holding discussions with their legal representatives and a few of the 'rebels' were determined not to let the matter rest.

I understand from discussions I have had since with some of the players involved and statements issued on their behalf that Gooch and Emburey were particularly upset about the severity of the punishment. My selection for England did not help.

Gooch was heard to comment more than once that he could not understand how he, born and raised just east of London, could be banned by England for going to play against South Africa when it was perfectly acceptable for England to pick somebody who was actually born in South Africa.

It was an argument which raised a great deal of sympathy throughout the country for the cause of the 'rebels' and there seems little doubt that if all cricket lovers were able to vote the outcome would have been strongly in favour of Gooch and his team.

There was nothing personal in Gooch's argument. As far as I am aware, he has had no objection to me playing for England apart from the unusual circumstances of his own case at the time. But I am sure it did not help my particular case and must have caused considerable resentment around the country among fans who saw my name in the England team when their own heroes were being denied the opportunity.

That argument has been raised a number of times since then. Some county members and various newspaper columnists have argued that the ban should have been reduced from three to two years, an argument which gained strength when England lost series in New Zealand and Pakistan for the first time during the early part of 1984. My name usually cropped up in those arguments.

Let me make it clear now that I did not agree with the ban, certainly not the length of it. I just obeyed the rules.

The popular view is that the ban was imposed on the 13 'rebels' to appease the major coloured cricketing playing nations and to avoid the threat of world cricket being split into two camps.

It was said, at the time, that if Gooch and Co went unpunished for playing against a South African national side outlawed by the International Cricket Conference, then India, Pakistan, the West Indies and Sri Lanka – only recently admitted to full ICC membership – would refuse to play against England. This, in the end, would result in a black international circuit made up of those countries leaving England, Australia and New Zealand to play among themselves.

It was also claimed – at the time – that the Test and County Cricket Board had been forced into taking the action they did only because both India and Pakistan were visiting England during the 1982 summer. If both pulled out of their scheduled commitments England would have been left without a Test series during that summer which would have left many county sides facing bankruptcy without a Test match income to keep them going.

It was also claimed – at the time – that if Australia had been scheduled to make a visit in 1982 and New Zealand in 1983 – as they were – no action would have been taken because there would not have been an immediate walk out by coloured playing countries and time heals all wounds.

Whatever the truth of the matter the majority of the people in this country appeared to believe that the TCCB had bowed down to threats from India, Pakistan and the West Indies, something they could not understand when India and Pakistan appeared happy to play against an England side containing me.

I hope that is not true for I believe it is wrong to bow down to outside pressure. English cricket must be run for the benefit of English cricket alone and I am not convinced there would have been a coloured walk out from the ICC if Gooch and Co had been allowed to continue as Test players.

The coloured playing countries need England and Australia on their circuit to provide them with money, particularly the West Indies. They would have recognised too that any walk out on their part would have kicked open the door – however slightly at the time – towards England, Australia and New Zealand re-establishing cricketing links with South Africa. Maybe South Africa could not tour those countries because cricketing grounds are difficult to protect but England could tour South Africa – and be richly rewarded – in the same way rugby teams from the British Isles continue touring.

In sympathising with Gooch and Co in the length of their ban from playing Test cricket, I do not think the claim many made that warnings issued by the TCCB were not clear enough holds water. It was certainly clear to me.

For some time it had been abundantly obvious that the South African cricketing authorities were contemplating a tour of this type. They had been quite open about it during 1981 after another failure to be given a hearing at the annual meeting at Lord's of the ICC. They announced then that they would listen to any scheme which might help keep the game alive at its highest level in their own country.

As a result every cricketer qualified to play for England or – in my case – about to be qualified, received a circular letter from the TCCB and signed by secretary D. B. Carr pointing out the danger of being involved in such a touring party.

It read:

> The Board understand that plans are being made to organise a team of international calibre to tour or to play a series of matches in South Africa in the near future.
>
> The Board wish to make it clear that any cricketer who takes part in any such international and/or representative match in South Africa could, thereby, make himself ineligible for future selection for England. Any cricketer who is unsure of the status that would be attributed to any match in which he is invited to take part should consult the Board through his county secretary, before accepting any such invitation.

Maybe the letter did not spell out in clear terms what any punishment would or could be. It was probably beyond the scope of the Board to do so at the time not knowing the exact nature of the tour and the proposed make-up of the opposition because of all the secrecy surrounding the venture.

There were legal implications too, players virtually being free agents once a season has finished and having a right to look for work as individuals during the off season. No player can afford to live for a year on his county salary alone.

But the mere fact that the Board found it necessary to issue a warning and the open invitation to have a private consultation with the Board should have sounded the alarm bells.

From the very first moment back in the early days of 1978 when it was first pointed out to me that I could become qualified for England after a four year waiting period, I made sure I never stepped out of line. I checked all my movements and out of season match commitments with Northants secretary Ken Turner before accepting any invitation.

I made sure that it was perfectly within the requirements of my qualification conditions that it was okay for me to continue my first class career in South Africa with Western Province, a side Gooch and Emburey were to join. I was back there helping them win the Currie Cup – South Africa's county championship – when the 'rebels' slipped into the country.

I had no idea they were there and no idea what was going on until I received a phone call from former South African Test player turned cricket official Ali Bacher asking me if I were available for selection for the South Africa side to play an England touring team. That was only a matter of weeks before I became qualified for England and I told him the same as I had told Joe Pamensky, President of the South African Cricket Union, two years earlier 'I'm sorry, I'm giving everything for England now.'

I had no interest in playing for South Africa when Joe had approached me which was long before my name was ever connected with a possible England place. I certainly wasn't going to spoil anything with that Ali Bacher phone call especially when it was followed almost immediately by a telegram from Ken Turner advising me not to have anything to do with those matches. I still have that telegram at home.

It was a pity all that controversy had been around at the time I was making my England bow which put my South African background more fully in the spotlight than it might have been. There was never the same reaction when, a year later, I was

31

8 Allan Lamb congratulates Pat 'Percy' Pocock on his first run for England in eight years during the Sri Lankan test at Lord's in August, 1984, in which Lamb made his fourth Test century of the season.

followed into the England side by another South African born batsman Chris Smith of Hampshire.

During the time the ban has been in force England have lost series to Australia, New Zealand, Pakistan and the West Indies. Coming out on the wrong side of those exchanges helped boost the number of calls for the ban to be reduced and the 'rebels' made free to pick up their Test careers in the belief their presence would have changed the results.

At various times over the last three years Gooch, Wayne Larkins, Dennis Amiss, Bob Woolmer and Peter Willey – not forgetting Geoff Boycott – have produced county innings that have made cricket lovers sigh for their presence again in the England side.

Yet, when I first entered the England side, I did not take a place that had been occupied by any of the 'rebels'! None of the middle order batsmen in the 'rebel' England XI had toured India and Sri Lanka during the 1981/82 winter immediately prior to their visit to South Africa.

It is possible, perhaps, that both my Northants' colleagues Peter Willey and Wayne Larkins might have been considered for the number three place I was to occupy when I first played for England if they had not been banned which did not make life too easy for me.

Although they never voiced any objection to me personally, they both felt as strongly as Gooch and Emburey about the presence of a South African born batsman in the England side when they were not allowed to play. It did result in some embarrassing moments in the Northants dressing room that summer whenever the South African subject was raised.

Looking at the England sides during that winter tour of India before the 'rebel' tour and the side chosen against India at home immediately afterwards, there were two basic changes in the middle order batting. Derek Randall was brought back to replace Mike Gatting at number six and I was called up to take over from Keith Fletcher who had lost the captaincy at the start of Peter May's term of office as chairman of selectors.

I state again that no 'rebel' lost his Test place or the £1,500 fee that goes with it because I was suddenly qualified. I stress that because it is a point many have conveniently overlooked since the actual event.

All the controversy surrounding the banning of the England players had one other side effect. I wasn't sure how I would be accepted by the other England players although Tony Greig appeared to be welcome when he had travelled along the same road 10 years earlier and Basil D'Oliveira had been greeted with open arms – two others born in South Africa.

Thankfully the greetings from the others appeared to be genuine enough when I first walked into an England dressing room for the start of the one day series against India and the Test matches to follow.

There was not the slightest hint of any animosity from any corner of the dressing room yet I still felt a little uneasy even at the end of my first summer for England by which time I had played in six Test matches and four one day internationals.

That feeling persisted when I left England that November to go on tour of Australia for the 1982–83 winter although, looking back, I suppose Norman Cowans must have felt even more uneasy.

He had risen to the top so quickly he had not even played a full season for Middlesex when he was chosen as England's rookie fast bowler. Consequently he did not really know any of the other 15 with him. Some he had not even met until we all assembled in London on the morning of our departure. It was even worse for Norman when he travelled. Normally we are all grouped together when we fly anywhere. On that flight there was a group of about 10 sitting together with the others spread around the tourist section and Norman was cut off from the main bunch.

To make sure that I was not cut off in any way I even sought an assurance from tour captain Bob Willis that I was wanted and fully accepted.

We had been in Australia for a fortnight and completed our first game by the time we arrived in Newcastle, the main industrial centre of northern New South Wales. I went out to lunch with Bob, David Gower and Ian Botham and over a marvellous dish of garlic prawns I asked the three of them if I fitted in. They seemed staggered that I should even raise the point.

I was grateful for their support that day. I have been tremendously grateful for the support all three of them have given to me ever since. They are another reason why I love playing for England.

Love it so much that, as proud as I am of the three centuries I scored against the West Indies in my attempt to become accepted by the public at large, I would willingly have swopped all of them for an England victory in the series against Clive Lloyd's remarkable team.

CHAPTER 3

A positive approach is the key

My father, Michael, was born in Walton-on-Thames, Surrey, of Irish stock, and although only a few people are aware of my connection with the Emerald Isle, those who are, insist that it explains why I am not averse to the odd tipple or two at the end of a day's play.

My mother, Joan, is English through and through and was born in Wembley on the northern approaches to London; and I just happen to have been born – and raised – in South Africa. *I* had no choice in the matter.

Neither had my parents had much choice, come to that; not that they are complaining, nor have they ever complained. Life has been good for them in South Africa, with my father enjoying a successful career with the South African Air Force, a career which came to an end with his retirement in 1984. And I also have many reasons to be grateful for having been raised there.

I arrived in this world in Langebaanweg – about an hour's drive from Cape Town – on 20th June 1954, and from the earliest times that I can remember sport has dominated my life. For a youngster with sporting ambitions to be raised in a land of almost constant sunshine, with only a brief winter, is a definite advantage, and I consider myself fortunate.

In such a climate much of life is spent out of doors. Swimming and running around on beaches are a part of growing up, not restricted to an annual holiday or the occasional day trip to the coast. And above all there is no huddling indoors, trying to keep warm, for almost half the year. Consequently the opportunities to play cricket, or other games, are far greater than in England. However I do wish that I had had the benefit of the English coaching system.

Australian and West Indian youngsters enjoy the same advantages, which is probably why they tend to be more natural athletes than the average youngster in England, and why they tend to mature as sportsmen at an earlier age than English kids do.

Having sampled the odd English winter and seen the limited *natural* facilities in this country, I find it perhaps rather surprising that England has produced so many outstanding performers in sports associated with, if not necessarily sunny, then at least, dry conditions.

Yet when England does produce a Seb Coe, a John Curry or even a Geoff Boycott they are world beaters, maybe because they have had to overcome so many obstacles in making their natural ability count.

I had no such hurdles to overcome except, perhaps, stiffer competition in that so many other youngsters of my age enjoyed the same climatic advantages and had the use of the abundant facilities those climatic conditions helped create.

I will hold my hands up now and admit that being white gave me the use of facilities which others of a different colour may not, at the time, have been able to enjoy. But I should also point out that the picture has changed dramatically in recent years, thanks – in the main – to the stand taken by South African cricketers of yesteryear.

From an early age I led an outdoor life, taking part in many sports. In the winter months Rugby was my main activity and eventually I developed into a reasonable fly-half or centre – in those days my legs could carry me across the ground with a fair turn of speed.

In the summer it was cricket, although tennis, squash and surfing also took up a fair bit of my time. I enjoyed them all, yet it was cricket which was to become my burning passion. I owe this to the encouragement I received from my father who was an enthusiastic cricketer and spent much of his spare time playing, either for a local club or in the services.

That is how I gained my introduction to the game, long before I started going to school. I was the youngest of four children. I have one sister living in England. She is married to Tony Bucknall, the former Richmond and England forward, thus adding to the family's sporting connections. I have another sister, living in

Johannesburg, where she controls a restaurant, and a brother who is a sales executive in furnishing, in Cape Town.

We are the product of the meeting in South Africa of two English families, both families having gone there for differing reasons. My father's folks had moved looking for a future at a time – sixty odd years ago – when South Africa was opening up and offering opportunities to anybody prepared to move and work hard.

My father himself was about to go to school when he was uprooted, and so he had his education in South Africa. The same applied to my mother, her family moving out in 1943 when her father was posted from Malta by the Royal Air Force.

Her family later moved back to England, but my mother stayed on having met my father by that time. Flying was his passion. A career in the South African Air Force beckoned, and in time included helping to defend the British Isles during the Second World War.

When peace returned my father became a fairly active cricketer and I would toddle after him when he played for the local country club, picking up any bat that was lying around, and playing about.

My game really started to develop when the family moved back to Cape Town when I was about five and then it made rapid progress when I joined Wynberg Boys' High School, where the schoolmasters gave me every encouragement.

It was about that time that I came under the influence of Tom Reddick, a former Notts player, who visited schools in the Western Province passing on his knowledge and wisdom. Tom did a marvellous job and many youngsters who went on to play first-class cricket for Western Province were schooled by him in the art of batsmanship. Basil D'Oliveira, who was born in Cape Town, was another pupil of Tom's, although before my time.

I also had the benefit of advice from many English county professionals, who used the winter break in their season at home to coach in South Africa. Sussex had very strong links with South Africa, and I can remember being advised by Don Bates, their former opening bowler and occasionally Alan Oakman, their former opening batsman who also played for England, who is now a coach at Warwickshire. Two others, later in my cricketing life, were David Steele and George Sharp; none of us realised then that we would team up together at Northampton.

George is a wicketkeeper and so was I early in my school

cricketing life, combining that role with opening the batting. I gave up wicketkeeping one day when we turned up for a match a bowler short. I volunteered to have a go with my swinging medium pace and finished up with six or seven wickets. From that moment onwards I became an all-rounder and still bowled for my local club, even when Western Province decided that my bowling was not fit to grace a first-class field. I can't say that I blame them.

But batting was my real love. I opened the innings for the school side and never wasted any time. If the bowling was short I hooked it. If it was well pitched up, I drove. The further the ball went, the better I liked it. Up and at 'em was my method and that is where good wicket conditions underfoot play such a vital part in the early days of a young cricketer.

I could generally afford to adopt that approach, knowing that I was playing on a good batting surface, where the ball came through evenly and usually held its line, enabling me to go for my shots. It distresses me when I see some of the wickets schoolboys have to use in this country – and not only schoolboys but first-class cricketers as well. It is hardly surprising that English cricket doesn't breed too many natural stroke-makers these days. It's become noticeable looking around the England dressing-room how many of the other occupants seem to come increasingly from public schools, where they have had the benefit of the best coaching and the best wicket conditions.

Throughout my cricketing life I have always believed in a positive approach to batting whenever possible, even though it has got me into trouble at times. I have no doubt that a few more of my half centuries would have been turned into three figures but for this aggressive approach. I've no doubt either that, in many instances, I would not have got any runs at all but for being prepared to take the bowler on.

My liking for hitting the ball always got me into trouble whenever I had a net session at school under the eye of Alan Oakman. He was teaching us how to play orthodox strokes; how to defend; and he always warned that anybody hitting the ball out of the net would be sent off immediately. If a ball came down that deserved to be hit – and even those that ought to have been treated with a greater measure of respect – I just couldn't resist having a go, whether it meant playing across the line or not. I never seemed

9   Allan Lamb reacts to a short ball from Imran Khan during the second Test at Lord's in 1982.

to spend more than a couple of minutes in the nets when Oakie was in charge.

The Lamb approach resulted in several early dismissals. It also resulted in plenty of runs, which took me into the school side and, eventually, the South African schools side. I was eighteen by then and earned myself a place in the Western Province team for a Nuffield sponsored week in Bulawayo, in Rhodesia – as it was then known, which brought together all the top schools players in the country.

The week ended with a South African schools side playing against Rhodesia. Rhodesia had a pretty strong Currie Cup side at the time, with their attack spearheaded by Mike Procter at his peak – both as a batsman and as a fast bowler. In addition they could boast of Jackie du Preez, Peter Carlstein and John Traicos (who had all played Test cricket for South Africa), Brian Davison – a colleague of Gower's at Leicestershire (who might have done) – and Robin Jackman who was on a winter break from Surrey.

It was during that match that I probably convinced Western Province's cricketing officials that my bowling had no place in the first-class game in South Africa. In fairness to myself I must state that my medium-paced swing-bowling was not called upon by the schools' captain until near the end of the Rhodesia innings when they were searching for runs. As I recall I had time for just four overs, which had resulted in a considerable amount of leather-hunting – by my team-mates – beyond the boundary edge. I think I must have gone for almost 50 runs in those four overs, far too many anyway for me ever to check accurately how many I had conceded. I know I didn't look for my bowling figures in the newspaper the next morning.

Batting was my main concern. I opened the innings and managed to see off the initial blitz from Procky. By the time I was approaching 30 runs on the board I felt I was going well. Probably too well, for I felt confident enough to have a go against the left-arm spin of Jimmy Mitchell and was out.

But even that stay at the wicket – brief as it was – must have convinced the Western Province selectors that I had something, for I was immediately selected to make my first-class debut early in 1973 against Eastern Province in the Currie Cup. My dream had come true. At least part of it had. For my dreams over the previous four or five years contained no limitations, and

41

involved county cricket in England even when I had just entered my teens.

I actually learned of my Western Province call-up from the newspapers, in the way we learn so much of what is happening to us in England – even confirmation of a Test place. This was an accident, however. On the three-day train journey home to Cape Town from Bulawayo, I bought a paper when the train stopped at a station somewhere on route. There was my name in the Western Province side and a couple of paragraphs announcing my first-class debut. I just hoped, for the rest of the journey, that the paper hadn't got it wrong.

It hadn't. The Western Province officials were at the station in Cape Town waiting to greet me with the news. It was a home match too – at Newlands where I had spent so many hours absolutely entranced by the activities of the players I was now to join.

And they were very good players, for Western Province had a strong side, although Natal and Transvaal had dominated the Currie Cup for a number of years and Western Province had not won the title outright since 1955/56. Eddie Barlow was the captain; he was a very inspiring leader, as Derbyshire were later to discover. The batting was strong – with him, Hylton Ackerman (another who played for Northants), Mike Bowditch, Sibley McAdam, Graham Chevelier and Andre Bruyns, with Peter Swart to help the bowling.

Eddie, of course, was very much a one-man band, as he demonstrated when he played for the Rest of the World in the series against England in 1970. He was a thoroughly dependable opening batsman, who never gave his wicket away but was not slow in scoring when he had the opportunity. He was a niggling medium-paced bowler, who could get everything there was to be had in a wicket as well as swing the ball, and a superb catcher. The other names might not be as familiar, but they would have been if South Africa had been a Test-playing country in the 1970s.

Above all Eddie wanted everything to run his way, which did not always please everybody, especially after his stint in first-class cricket in England when he had realised that playing the game seven days a week, throughout a four month season, demanded fitness of the highest level.

The Derbyshire players have told me how Eddie had them

running miles in pre-season practice, and running and exercising before each day's play in the summer. He demanded fitness of the highest order, which had not pleased too many Derbyshire players when he first assumed the captaincy during the 1976 season in England. A year later, however, they were swearing by him and his ideas when they realised how much better they felt for it, and how their individual – and team – performances had improved.

Seeing how much Derbyshire had improved, Eddie returned to Cape Town each winter determined to make the Western Province players the fittest in the Currie Cup. And that did not go down too well either. At least it didn't with some of the older players, and I was left with the impression that two or three of them dropped out of Western Province quicker than they might otherwise have done because of the fitness regime Eddie imposed. They would argue that playing only eight Currie Cup first-class matches each season plus a one-day competition did not demand the same high physical standards as English cricket. Eddie would argue that it was essential to be in peak physical condition for every top-class game.

And I argued too, even as a youngster: not deliberately, not to challenge his authority, not to show-off, but simply because I have never been one to keep quiet. Perhaps argue is too strong a word. It was just that I could never seem to remain silent and was always chipping in with a comment, the cheekier the better, at a time when young men were supposed to sit quietly in the corner of the dressing-room and become 'doers' for the more experienced and senior players who were demanding 'do this' or 'do that'.

I never stopped admiring Eddie all the time I played with him. His own physical make-up made it difficult for him to appear a fleet-footed athlete. He was a stocky-looking figure, as you might expect of a farmer – tremendously thick arms; a barrel of a chest on a solid frame; finished off by short, thick legs that would carry him through over after over in the most humid of conditions without his ever showing any signs of distress. Yet, despite his appearance, he was as fit and as tough as the next man in the side.

Although I admired him, we were never the greatest of pals and I could understand his not being too impressed by my cheeky outlook from the very first time we batted together in my first-class debut against Eastern Province.

Eddie opened the innings and I went in at number three, soon teaming up with him in a second-wicket partnership. I was nicknamed the 'Happy Hooker' in those days. As I've already said, if anybody bowled short at me they had to go no matter what. Before the innings Eddie had warned me it would be far tougher than any other cricket I had known. I would be playing with men, not boys, and I should curb my natural instincts a little in order to work things out and survive.

His words of wisdom were forgotten the moment the ball was dropped short, soon after I arrived at the crease. I went for the hook, missed and looked up to find Eddie advancing towards me down the wicket. 'They have placed a man on the boundary ready for the hook shot,' he said. 'Don't do it.'

Knowing what I know now, I'd say he was right; that is the type of advice I would feed to any youngster who looked like being carried away on his debut. At the time I was a little put out. I had my chance the very next over.

This time it was Eddie who went for a hook shot, getting a four as well, the ball travelling too fiercely for any fielder to get a hand to it – dangerous yet safe. While the ball was being recovered *I* strolled down the wicket – an eighteen-year-old, playing his first Currie Cup match, approaching a man who had played thirty times for his country, was my provincial captain and was recognised as one of the world's finest all-rounders. 'Remember that man on the boundary?' I said. 'He's there to catch you as well.' And I walked back to the bowler's end. Eddie was speechless.

I stayed in long enough to score a half century in the first innings and followed with an innings of 36 the second time around. This was good enough to get me into the Western Province side again for the next match against Natal at their Kingsmead ground. I quickly learned there that Eddie had been right in his words in my first game.

The wicket was a bit of a green top and the other players in the Western Province side warned me that I would find it a little quicker and bouncier than what I had been used to in Cape Town. They warned me, too, that I could expect no mercy from the Natal bowlers, who would first try to discover how brave I was before deciding whether I was any good as a batsman.

Vincent van der Bijl was the bowler when I went to the crease; the gentle giant who helped Middlesex win the county championship and the Gillette Cup in 1980, took them to third place in the John Player League, and the semi-finals of the Benson and Hedges Cup. Mike Brearley said afterwards that Vincent had been 'the greatest single factor' in Middlesex's triumph by the way he teased batsmen mercilessly on wickets which gave him any assistance – not that Vincent ever needed too much help. He would bring the ball down from around the nine foot mark with a deceptive change of pace, his faster ball getting up off just short of a length, yet so well disguised in delivery that batsmen were usually well committed to their stroke when suddenly forced to defend desperately around the rib region. He was amazingly accurate, too, no less than 49 of his 85 championship victims that summer being bowled or leg before.

Greenhorn Lamb knew of Vincent by name but nothing of his remarkable skill. Sure enough the first ball he served me was a bouncer. Remembering the words of my colleagues I decided to ignore it. I watched it pitch short, ducked underneath it and watched it go through at around what would have been shoulder height had I been standing upright. And, I thought, at a lovely slow pace. Right, I said to myself, if that is the best he can do for a bouncer on what is supposed to be a quick wicket, the ball is going right out of the park next time he drops it short.

The next time was the very next delivery. The same action, the same spot on the wicket. A six for the taking and a nice way to get off the mark. Or so I thought. No ducking this time. I went for the hook but was still only half-way through my stroke when the ball found the top edge and smashed into my forehead. Blood spurted and off I went for seven stitches.

I can't remember looking back at Vincent's face but I have no doubt there was a little smile playing around his lips. Another sucker in the bag. I'd fallen into his trap but it had proved a valuable lesson. I learned that no two balls which looked the same, reacted the same way even if they appeared to be bowled with identical actions and pitched on the same spot.

Vincent was a master. I remember Keith Pont, Essex's medium-paced all-rounder, telling me of his experience when facing Vincent in 1980 on a Southend wicket, which is not always true at the best of times. This one was rain-affected and Vincent finished the match with figures of eight for 65 from 51.3 overs in Middlesex's eight-wicket win towards their championship title.

10   Catching flies while scoring 137 n.o. against New Zealand at Trent Bridge in August 1983.

11   Lamb against Hadlee in the third Test at Auckland in February, 1984.

Keith was not a Vincent victim. In fact he was Essex's top scorer with 36 in their first innings.

Yet he remembers facing one over from Vincent in which he played at every delivery without once managing to put his bat against the ball. 'At the end of the over Vincent came down the wicket to me and asked what I thought I was doing out in the middle. I had to confess to him that I had no idea,' said Keith.

My first meeting with Vincent early in 1973 happened to be my last experience of first-class cricket for a couple of years. I did return to the crease right at the death of the Western Province innings, with my forehead decorated by a neat piece of stitching, but the innings was soon over. I never got another chance because we beat Natal by an innings.

Western Province still had a couple of matches to play that season but it was exam time for me and I couldn't take the time off from school. Before the next Currie Cup season started in 1973/74 I was away doing my two year's National Service. It was strictly country district for me during that period.

I could have played first-class cricket if I had stayed in Pretoria. Being a sportsman in the services has many advantages, and every opportunity was placed before me to get time off from official duties to enable me to play. But I did not like Pretoria. I wanted a posting as near to Cape Town as possible, although it meant sacrificing the opportunity of staying in the first-class game.

I ended up in a place called George, which is about an eight-hour car drive to Cape Town, too far to participate in Western Province cricket. I was a plant operator for eighteen months, driving tractors and huge earth-moving equipment, building a new airport.

Yet those two matches that I had played in had taught me a lot, and helped me to survive when I returned two years later, by which time – for the first time in fifteen years – Western Province had, in 1974/75, won the Currie Cup outright. The following seasons we were the target that every other side was trying to bring down.

They play it hard in South Africa, harder than in county cricket in England. There is no mercy shown. If, after getting one or two past the edge, a bowler doesn't think you can bat, he'll let you know in no uncertain terms, so will the close in fielders. There is always a lot of chatting going on, most of it derogatory as far as the batsman is concerned. You quickly have to learn to give as good as you get, otherwise you are doomed. I was always able to look after myself in that department, right from the very start, but I have known players who cracked under the verbal intimidation. Anyway two years in the National Service had taught me a few new words to hurl back whenever anybody had a go at me.

There was a very hard school of players about. Some of them were bitter also, having been denied the chance to express themselves at the very highest level. I think it is commonly accepted that South Africa would have been THE Test team of the late 1960s and the early 1970s had they been playing international cricket regularly. And who knows what might have gone on from there?

Some of the greatest players the country has ever produced had just started to blossom to their full glory when the Basil D'Oliveira affair broke in 1968. South Africa were outlawed as a Test-playing nation for refusing to accept a lightly coloured man, born in Cape Town, as a member of the England side for the scheduled 1968/69 tour. South Africa were to play only one other series, entertaining Australia in 1969/70 and thrashing them 4–0, before the rest of the cricketing world spurned them.

As well as the great new names such as the Pollock brothers, Graeme and Peter, Ali Bacher, Eddie Barlow, Mike Procter and Barry Richards, there were others who were beginning to come into the picture. Two of them played for Western Province and were to have a great influence on my cricketing life. Garth Le Roux, the giant fast bowler with Sussex, who found his fame as a pin-up destroyer of batsmen with the Kerry Packer circus, was one. Peter Kirsten, who reeled off century after century for Derbyshire during his five years with them, was the other.

Both are a year younger than I am. Garth, in fact, went to the same school in Cape Town (Wynburg Boys' High) as I did, but the boy I had known there is completely unrecognisable in the bowler who patrols the Hove ground today with his giant strides.

Garth, as a fifteen- or sixteen-year-old, was a little titch. He was also an off-spinner in those days. We nicknamed him 'Jim' after Jim Laker, and the larger boys used to bully him a little in the nets. I include myself in that group of larger boys because, although I myself stood only 5ft 6in or so at the time, I could still see over the top of Garth's head when I stood next to him!

12   A rare moment of concentration on the balcony at Lord's, July 1982.

He suffered at my hands one day whilst we were still at school together. Not far away from us was a girls school, and I can remember leading a small group who grabbed Garth, stripped him down to his underpants and tied him up to some railings where the girls could not fail to spot him when they left the school grounds. How Garth suffered!

That story got around, which probably explains what happened to me after I was cheeky to the senior Western Province players during my second first-class match against Natal at Kingsmead – the one where I collected a forehead scar by courtesy of Vincent van der Bijl.

To get their own back after I had refused to bow down and keep quiet as they expected all newcomers to behave, they turned on me later in the season during a game against Rhodesia in Bulawayo. The lads borrowed a pair of handcuffs from a friendly policeman, stripped me naked and chained me to some railings outside the ground – walking off with the key. It was some time before they returned and set me free. By which time I'd been the target of some pointed ribbing from all the passers-by.

I did not see much of Garth during those early days, although I glimpsed him occasionally when I returned to Wynburg to play in odd matches against the school side, by which time Garth had started to grow and had turned himself into a useful fast bowler, or possibly more medium pace in those days.

By the time I was back playing for Western Province again Garth had gone away to do *his* National Service. What a shock it was when he did return! He seemed to have done all his growing in those two years and he came back to us topping 6ft 3in – and very fast. There was no question of my ever tangling with him again or trying to strip him down to his underpants. And he has found a way of getting his own back – I've had to contend with many a bouncer whistling past my ears.

Peter, who was actually born in Pietermaritzburg, Natal, but went to school in Cape Town, made a name for himself when he made his first-class debut the first year I was away with the Army.

In a way he had taken my place in the Western Province side and was an immediate hit, going on to shatter records for Western Province and with Derbyshire. During the 1976/77 season, for instance, he set a record of five centuries in a Currie Cup season, which is some going even considering the marvellous batsmen

South Africa has produced over the years. Four of those centuries were made in succession.

Needless to say he set a Western Province scoring record that summer, of 967 runs with an average of 76, and he also became the first batsman to score ten centuries for Western Province. His record-breaking did not end there, for he set a new Derbyshire record in 1982 of eight centuries in the summer having, in 1980, the Derbyshire record of four double centuries in a season, three of them undefeated.

He was a dynamic little batsman, who became the batting hero of Western Province at the same time as Garth Le Roux was beginning to knock over the opposition in double quick time to become the fast-bowling hero.

As a result the pair of them gained a scholarship, through Western Province, to spend the summer of 1977 in England to broaden their experience, Peter having already spent a couple of seasons in England when having a few games for Sussex, including playing against the 1975 Australians.

I must admit I was a little jealous – more than a little. I was envious. As I stated earlier, it had always been my dream to play county cricket in England, but on the wages I earned, selling timber for a firm in Cape Town, I could not possibly afford the passage. I needed an assisted passage if I were going to get to England, but nobody had heard of me in this country. Nobody was able to assist me.

That's where my uncle Peter, who lives in Johannesburg, stepped in. He knew of my desire. The whole family knew of it. It may even have been to shut me up that, provided I could fend for myself once in England, Uncle Peter agreed to pay my air passage.

When the offer was made I did not even bother to wonder how I would exist. I just jumped at the chance. And when Peter Kirsten and Garth le Roux, their pockets stuffed full of contacts provided for them by Eddie Barlow, left Cape Town to go to Derbyshire, I trooped along with them.

It was the start of the journey that was to turn me into an Englishman.

CHAPTER 4

The South African question

I can't honestly say whether I would now be playing for England or not if South Africa had not been outlawed as a Test-playing nation back in the late 1960's, following their treatment of Basil D'Oliveira. I suspect I would be, unless South Africa had grabbed hold of me before 1977. But I was never faced with the problem of choosing one country before another, as were Roland Butcher and Norman Cowans when they put England before the West Indies.

Playing for England was the last thing on my mind when, determined to find a cricketing future, I linked up with Peter Kirsten and Garth Le Roux and arrived in England shortly before the 1977 County Championship season. I had no idea, at that stage, that there was ever any chance of my playing Test cricket for anybody.

Playing *county* cricket was on my mind. It dominated most of my thinking. It had been a deep longing, ever since the days when, as a schoolboy, I had read avidly about cricket in every newspaper or magazine on which I could lay my hands, and the game had begun to dominate my life.

More specifically, during that period, I had lapped up every report I could find detailing the exploits in county cricket of Barry Richards (Hampshire), Mike Procter (Gloucestershire), Lee Irvine (Essex), Hylton Ackerman (Northants), Brian Davison (Leicestershire), Tony Greig (Sussex) and a few others: South Africans all. All appeared to be very successful – and South Africa is very proud of its sporting heroes. Consequently their deeds were given extensive coverage in South African newspapers, centuries earning many column inches, feature articles and pictures decorating many pages. A fine innings by, say, Richards would be more extensively reported in South Africa than in any English news-paper. Looking back it was a way, I suppose, of demonstrating to the general public in South Africa that their cricketers were the tops, even if they could not play together as a team and prove it.

I envied each and every one of them when I was a schoolkid and a strong desire built up inside me then to try and emulate them when I grew older. They appeared giants of the game from such a vast distance. Later, when I graduated into the Western Province side and was able to listen to stories of English county cricket at first hand, my appetite became even stronger.

As a schoolboy I knew nothing about the rules and qualification regulations, especially those governing selection to the England side. It did not even occur to me that I was different from most others playing cricket in South Africa, or those South Africans playing in county cricket, in that both my parents were English.

It did not even occur to me to inquire how Tony Greig, who was born in Queenstown, South Africa and had served his cricketing apprenticeship with Border and Eastern Province in the Currie Cup, had managed to get into the England side. He was first selected to play against the Australians in 1972. At that time I was just coming up to eighteen, was still at school, had not made my first-class debut, and my immediate horizon was obscured by thoughts of spending two years doing my National Service.

Some five years later when I arrived in England I was still unaware of the possibilities that could open up for me. All that concerned me during the year 1977 was to create, through my batting ability, an impression good enough to attract a county side, who might then give me an opportunity from the following summer onwards. I left England six months later a sad and disappointed young man.

Nobody had stepped forward and grabbed me. One or two expressed some interest after Derbyshire had notified all other sixteen first-class counties that they had a couple of promising South African batsmen based with them for the season. I played a couple of second-eleven matches for Lancashire, a few more for Northants. I also turned out for Derryck Robins' XI along with Imran Khan, who was waiting for his clearance to play for Sussex after having left Worcestershire. On that second-eleven circuit I first met up with Allan Border, who was spending the 1977 summer in England along with fellow Australian Dave Whatmore.

Derbyshire gave me a few second-eleven matches as well, and I also turned out fairly regularly for Holmfirth in the Huddersfield League, but I returned to Cape Town at the end of that summer without one concrete offer.

Yet eventually the visit turned out not to have been a waste of time. One discovery was made that summer which was to pave the way into the England team and prove an attraction as far as Northants were concerned. I have David Harrison, then secretary of Derbyshire, to thank for that.

He was the man who discovered that I was 'another Greig'. In talking to me early that summer and discussing my background, he found out that both my parents had been born in England. He promptly checked the qualification rules and learned that I could be regarded as 'English' for qualification purposes – within four years of being registered with a county side – as long as I observed all the other conditions laid down by the Test and County Cricket Board.

I am not sure how Northants found out. Possibly when Ken Turner, their secretary/manager, attempted to sign up Peter Kirsten, only to discover that Derbyshire had beaten them to my Western Province partner for the 1978 season onwards. Instead they turned to me, the added attraction being that my English parentage would give them the freedom to play an additional overseas-born player in their first team from 1982 onwards, if they felt they needed one.

It was just before Christmas, 1977, that I got the best present I had ever received. The late Mr Roy Barker, a Northants committee-man in the shoe trade, flew to South Africa on business, but combined the trip with talking to my early coach Tom Reddick and then offering me the chance to join the county. The money did not really matter at the time. I can't remember having second thoughts. This was the opportunity I had been seeking to be able to copy the Richards, Procters and Irvines. It meant walking out on my employers in Cape Town who had been very good to me. They were full of understanding once again, and agreed to release me when the time came for me to fly to England.

It was only then that my England ambitions were well and truly fired. Secretary Turner, my mentor throughout my early years in English cricket, explained what might be possible as long as I fulfilled all the requirements, including agreeing to transfer my home to England. I did not need any prompting to say yes, and to start the procedure towards gaining British citizenship.

From that moment onwards the only thing which interested me was runs, runs and still more runs. I felt I needed to show the people in Northampton – and the team – that they had not signed a no-hoper. I wanted to convince people right from the start that I could play – might even be a little better than most – so that they would start putting my name forward before the selectors, ready for the time in 1982 when I would be eligible for an England call-up.

I got 883 in my first summer from seventeen matches, which was good enough to top the Northants averages with 46.47 and earn me my county cap, although my season was to end before the summer was out. It was Wayne Daniel, Middlesex's West Indian Test fast bowler, who put an end to it and also ruined a day I had dreamed about for years – playing first-class cricket at Lord's, the head-quarters of the world game.

It was supposed to be a memorable occasion, a time to soak up the atmosphere of the most famous ground in the world, although the crowd was thin, and the stands almost empty. And it still was an occasion as far as I was concerned: going into the visitors' dressing room – the one on the right as you look at the pavilion. It's a large, sparse room with coat hooks around the walls, a couple of sinks, two or three arm chairs, benches and a huge table in the middle, plus the 'coffins' – the trunk-like suitcases all cricketers use in which to carry their gear. The showers are in a corridor outside which means you have to nip in and out, avoiding members going up or coming down from the top balcony. Hardly luxurious, certainly inconvenient, but I was not to care.

Then there is the walk down two flights of steps, through the famous Long Room, and then through the middle doors when going out to bat. You walk past portraits of famous cricketers gazing down on the members themselves, some of whom ignore you completely, others look at you with idle curiosity, still more with envious eyes, wishing that they had the talent to be in your place.

I had dreamed about returning past those same members with a century under the belt, but that was not to be. I returned with my right hand racked with pain, a finger broken by a Daniel delivery, which put me out for the final month. I missed another ten innings or so during which I might have got close to the 1,500 target I had set to announce myself.

At least I had arrived and more or less survived. My cricket had been given a new meaning and purpose. Even a chance of a Test future if I could build on those beginnings over the next three seasons. I was one of the fortunate ones from South Africa.

For the great majority of youngsters who had picked up a cricket bat for the first time about the period I was beginning to wave mine around, there was no such future. And, I suspect, for the hundreds of youngsters who are about to pick up a cricket bat on the boundary edge while their fathers are playing a club game out in the middle, there will be no such future either.

Speaking purely from a cricketing viewpoint, the decision in 1969 by the International Cricket Conference at Lord's to make South Africa Test outcasts, was a tragic one. It robbed cricket-lovers around the world – and I include those in the Caribbean, Pakistan and India – of watching some of the greatest talent the game has produced.

I am not going to enter into the political issue. I am not naïve enough to say that sport and politics should not mix. In an ideal world they would not. But this is not an ideal world. Such mixing, however, should be kept to a bare minimum, because most politicians are not equipped to speak on behalf of sport or understand the problems of the game. At the same time I, as a sportsman, am not equipped to interfere on the political front, not being privy to all the facts which explain the decisions that are taken.

I do know that all the requirements, laid down on South Africa's doorstep when they were first expelled from the ICC as a condition for their re-admittance, have been carried out. Black and white do play freely together on the cricket fields now. And I have never known any other cricketing way of life as a senior player.

My club, Green Point, in Cape Town were the first to go multi-racial. It had black members in it from the moment I joined them, and Western Province have enjoyed the spinning services of coloured Omar Henry, who has also played for Scotland in the Benson and Hedges Cup. But, then again, Cape Town has always been a little more liberal than many other areas in South Africa, because of the English rather than the Dutch Afrikaans influence.

The South African Cricket Union, the old white-dominated

body, has done everything in its power to make cricket in the country multi-racial and has achieved far more over the last ten years than ninety-nine per cent of the people would have expected.

Their cricket is open to anybody whatever their colour. Local leagues have been organised on a multi-racial pattern, even primary leagues for schoolchildren. Social barriers, once so strict and rigid, have been pushed back, changes made in the Liquor Act so that all races can eat and drink together in sports clubs; white and black can change together. A great deal of money has been spent, too, on importing coaches, whose experience and guidance is available to all groups.

With such changes it is not surprising that members of the South African Cricket Union feel let down by the refusal of the ICC to keep their re-admittance promise, or even give them an official hearing at their annual meeting at Lord's.

If there are not more blacks playing cricket and taking advantage of the opportunities open to them, it is the fault of the South African Cricket Board which represents the black community, rather than of the Cape Coloured or the Asian groups. They refuse to co-operate, even objecting strongly to any black who ignores their teachings and insists on fulfilling a cricketing ambition.

I don't think it is helping their people, but I can understand their sentiments. Apartheid is a horrible and very emotive word. The anti-apartheid bodies have right on their side when they say that, in a world where everybody is supposed to be born with equal opportunity and rights, the freedom to mix openly on the sporting fields is not enough. They want the freedom won by cricket to extend to every walk of life, every job and every situation. That is still light years away in South Africa.

Such cricketing freedom as the Asians, the Cape Coloureds, and the blacks who risk the wrath of their brothers have won, is due in large part to the courage of those white Test players who started the moves to make the game multi-racial almost as soon as the ICC ban was implemented.

These players included Eddie Barlow, Mike Procter and the Pollock brothers, who staged their own demonstration in favour of throwing the game wide open when they walked off the field during a trial match in 1971. The trial was being held to help the

South African selectors find a Springbok side scheduled to visit Australia later that year. The tour, of course, was cancelled.

These men, and others like them, had tasted Test cricket. They knew the changes they were insisting upon to satisfy the ICC conditions would never be implemented quickly enough for them ever to play Test cricket again. But they were determined to get the movement started, by defying officials and organisations, so that their children, and their children's children, might enjoy Test cricket, whether as spectators or players.

But, with each concession their movement won, so fresh demands were made for even more barriers to come down. I can't see that situation changing for many years to come, despite the presence in London now of my former captain Barlow. He is on a mission sponsored by the cricket, rugby and Olympic bodies to try to explain to the rest of the world what changes have taken place in South Africa, and the extent of the victories won. Those bodies could not have made a better choice, for Eddie is firmly committed to bringing down every barrier.

I know that if I were a youngster in South Africa today, with more than average talent for ball games, I would undoubtedly be turning away from cricket and organised team games. I would want to concentrate on golf, tennis, squash or any other individual sport where it is still possible for a South African to compete at a world level and prove himself against the best in the world.

Even for people like myself, Tony Greig, Chris and Robin Smith (who play for Hampshire), the door is beginning to close as far as England is concerned. Early in 1984 the Test and County Cricket Board approved much tougher and harsher qualification rules to make it more difficult for South-African-born cricketers of English parents ever to play for England. I hope that is not a direct result of me or Chris Smith managing to get into the England side, or of anticipation that Chris' younger brother Robin should do within the next year or so.

I have been assured that it is nothing personal but is in order to tighten up any loopholes which county clubs might wriggle through when all county sides are restricted to fielding only one 'non England' qualified player before the end of the 1980s. When this policy was approved by the TCCB in 1983, there was a fear that some county sides might try to get round it by signing other South-African-born cricketers of English parents so that they could get them registered as 'English' by 1988 or 1989 and include them and, say, a West Indian test cricketer in the first team at the same time.

Right until the end of the 1981/82 season I continued to play Currie Cup cricket for Western Province and I believe I detected a slight fall in the standard of South African domestic cricket. There is no doubt, in my opinion, that their game has lost some good and talented players because they have not been able to see a Test-playing future.

Although I was not old enough at the time to appreciate the situation, I get the impression from talking to others that some players, right at their peak when the ICC ban was implemented, dropped out of cricket earlier than they might otherwise have done in order to concentrate on their business futures.

There has been enough evidence over the years to suggest that South Africa has been a cricketing gold mine, with the emergence of such talented players at Kenny McEwan, Clive Rice, Peter Kirsten, Lee Irvine, Hylton Ackerman, Vincent van der Bijl and Garth Le Roux. All have left their mark on the county scene in England; and their mark is a pretty indelible one too.

For everyone who has made the grade over here – and most of the ones I have mentioned are – or were – either the best or the second best player in their respective county sides, there are others back in South Africa who could have done the same if they had chosen cricket as a full-time career rather than going for a business future and playing cricket as a spare time, weekend hobby.

And I can't help wondering how much better players, such as those I have mentioned (as good as they are now), might have been had they been faced with the challenge of playing Test cricket.

One or two of them, owing to defects of temperament, might not have survived at the highest level, even though they have proved themselves in the toughest domestic circuit in the world. There is a vast difference between county cricket and that at a Test level. If they had come through, they would certainly have been improved.

There is something missing from their cricketing lives. They have tasted a little of what it is like in playing for South Africa against the rebel sides from England, the West Indies and Sri

Lanka. But they were not top-class sides and there is no substitute for the real thing.

It is a tragedy for them, for they have done nothing wrong as individuals. It is a tragedy, too, that spectators have not been able to enjoy watching them compete at the highest level. Just as it is sad that all cricket-watchers have not been able to enjoy the rich ability of Graeme Pollock or Barry Richards.

Pollock is far and away the best left-handed batsman I have ever seen. I don't think I have ever watched anybody hit the ball so hard and yet be so classically orthodox at the same time. He produced a combination of a Colin Cowdrey cover-drive played with all the power of Ian Botham.

Most hitters tend to be sloggers as well, just because of the extra weight and power they put into their strokes. Pollock never was. His timing was so perfect when he was at his peak that he needed only to lean into a delivery with his heavy bat to send the ball scudding through the outfield to the boundary. Yet he still hit the ball with a full flourish of the bat as well.

He had a great economy of movement with his rather widish stance, seldom indulging in elaborate footwork except when going down the wicket against a spinner. Perhaps his right foot – the leading foot in his case – would move an inch or two down the wicket to help him get to the pitch of a delivery just short of a length. Yet he was so well balanced, he could quickly rock on to his back foot, all in the same movement, to deal with a ball shorter than he expected.

Barry Richards was something else. He just had everything. With his marvellous eye I do not think there was a stroke he could not play to perfection. It was, however, his cover-driving which sent coaches into raptures, and thousands away ecstatic, when he produced a few of them in one of his long innings. He was so good; found it all so easy, that boredom became his greatest enemy at the crease. That was the only thing which stopped him scoring more centuries than he might otherwise have done.

He was a player who needed the challenge of Test cricket to bring out the very best in him. I understand that he used to play make-believe Test matches in his own mind during his seasons with Hampshire, in order to get him through a summer without being too careless.

Having been brought up to playing a first-class match in the

Currie Cup only every now and again, with plenty of time to prepare himself mentally for every big match, he found the daily routine of English county cricket rather a hard grind once he had proved himself the best opening batsman of his time. I am told he would study the fixture list at the start of a Hampshire season and select half a dozen of the most challenging attacks he most wished to conquer. These county games would become his Test matches.

The other county matches in between were the equivalent of the club games he would have been playing back at home, games he could rest in mentally, although still doing a good job for his county whilst building himself up to take on Yorkshire, Middlesex or whoever were the strongest county of his day. I doubt whether he failed often in those matches, while Hampshire's games against the touring sides always held a fascination for him, providing the opportunity to take on an international attack.

Eddie Barlow was another Richards-like figure in that respect. He had proved such an inspiration as a leader with Western Province because he would often announce beforehand just what he was going to do – and then go out and do it. He would wander into the dressing-room and tell us 'I think I'll score a century today.' Then he would march out and do just that. Or, in the field, he would put himself on with his swinging medium pace and say 'I'm going to take a wicket now.' Again he would do just that.

South Africa's cricket was, of course, badly hit during the three years that the Kerry Packer circus was in operation in Australia and before the television tycoon and the Australian cricketing authorities made peace and teamed up together.

Both being in the Southern Hemisphere, the cricket seasons in Australia and South Africa are at the same time of the year. It meant that the Currie Cup competition lost the likes of Barlow, Procter, Le Roux, Richards and Rice. Their absence upset a considerable number of people in South Africa who believed they should have stayed at home.

I did not blame them at all. In my book, they were less guilty than the Australia, West Indies and England players involved who deliberately went against their official authorities and cut themselves off from Test cricket. For the South Africans the circus provided them with a chance to demonstrate their ability to live and play with the best in the world.

Having now played against every Test-playing country, and

having returned most winters to play in the Currie Cup until I became eligible for England, I have no hesitation in saying that for most of the last fifteen years or so, South Africa would have been either the best Test side or a very close second to the West Indies.

They might have struggled for a series in the mid 1970s, when Dennis Lillee was at his peak and Jeff Thomson teamed up with him under Greg Chappell's Australian command. Still I believe they had the batsmen to cope at the time, as well as an attack – spearheaded by Mike Procter – to bowl the Australians out.

They might have struggled against the first great West Indies all-pace attack of Andy Roberts, Michael Holding, Joel Garner and Colin Croft, but such a meeting would have produced some titanic battles that would have enriched the game of cricket.

Today it might be a little different. There is not quite the bowling strength around in South Africa to be able to command Viv Richards and company, although the batting might just fare a little better than that of other countries has done of late. I get the impression that, as a result of not being able to offer a Test-playing future, South African cricket is not as talent-laden as it once was. That is a great pity.

CHAPTER 5

The Australians owe me a Test century

The Aussies owe me a Test century. Ever since I bade them farewell, after the end of the 1982/83 series over there, I've been itching to get my bat on their bowling again, in the return encounter – but with home advantage – in 1985.

I should have taken two, possibly three, centuries off them that winter. If it had been three, they would have been in successive Tests just as they were against the West Indies. And, if I had done that, perhaps England would have been defending the Ashes this summer instead of trying to get them back.

Yes, I'm afraid I missed out on that 1982/83 winter. In the second Test of that tour in Brisbane I was 28 runs short of reaching three figures in the England first innings when I was out to an astonishing catch. At least I was astonished. I believe Rod Marsh was too by the look of sheer joy on his face when he finished his run and acrobatic leap to hold on to the catch. We lost that Test by seven wickets.

A fortnight or so later, in Adelaide in the third Test, I was even closer to a century I had worked hard to get. I was only 18 runs away this time when Marshy caught me again. There was an element of disagreement about that dismissal. I was convinced I had not touched the ball when I aimed a pull against Geoff Lawson. Umpire Mel Johnson was convinced I had. There is only one winner in that situation. It wasn't me, although I accept you have to take the rough with the smooth when it comes to decisions.

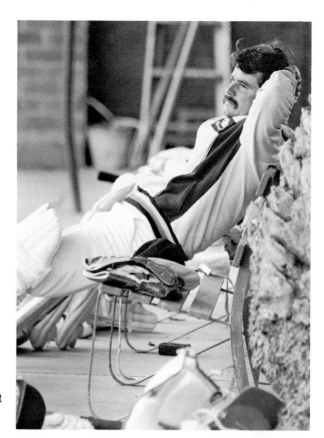

13 Reflecting on those missed centuries in the opening two Tests against Australia at the Adelaide ground, December, 1982.

At Melbourne between Christmas and New Year I was one run closer still towards three figures. With only 17 wanted when I was caught, it really had been there for the taking. Missing out then was down to me. I played a rash and undisciplined shot and holed out. Rush of blood, they call it.

My disappointment quickly evaporated when we won that match by three breath-taking, heart-stopping runs on the back of some fine fast bowling from Norman 'Flash' Cowans. This put us back in the series with a chance of drawing it – good enough to keep the Ashes. Unfortunately there was no fairy-tale ending to the final Test in Sydney.

Things went from bad to worse after that. We messed up our challenge in the one-day triangular series which followed, when the other participants – Australia and New Zealand – both clearly feared us. Our downfall was in thinking that the 296 for five we scored against New Zealand in Adelaide in a qualifying round was way beyond the capabilities of Geoff Howarth's side over fifty overs. We did not think we could possibly lose – even when Lance Cairns and Richard Hadlee started smashing us to pieces – until it was too late to apply the brake.

Victory in that match would have put us through to the finals. Instead we lost to New Zealand again, which left us kicking our heels in Sydney for ten days while the other two contested the honours. By the time we travelled on to New Zealand for three one-day games on a leg of a tour that should never have been arranged, we were in no mood for picking up the pieces after four months away. We were easy meat for New Zealand in all three games.

Losing out in all competitions, coupled with my failure to score a Test century, resulted in my returning home feeling very frustrated, especially as it had been my first overseas tour for England. Overall I was satisfied with the standard of my performance, but I will not be happy until England holds the Ashes again and I have taken at least one Test century off the Aussies. If I could score that century in helping England regain the Ashes, so much the better. Perhaps then, I shall be completely accepted by the general public for what I am – an England batsman; full stop. The summer of 1985 could be an important one for me.

I also hope very much that England's batsmen, thanks to moves we started on that tour in which I had much to say, will be better equipped to take on the Australian fast bowlers. If that is so, the experience in losing that series 2–1 will not have been entirely wasted.

From captain Bob Willis downwards, we all came back absolutely determined that the ridiculous one-bouncer-per-over limitation experimental rule in English county cricket must be scrapped. It had to be if England were to stand any chance in future of competing as equals against other international attacks boasting of a four-man pace battery.

Even manager Doug Insole must have been convinced we were right after watching us being peppered throughout that series by as many as four short-pitched deliveries per over, particularly when the likes of Lawson, Rodney Hogg and Jeff Thomson came across a bouncier than normal wicket, as they did in Brisbane. They had a ball. It was no fun for those of us attending it.

Coming from a summer in England, in which fast bowlers in county cricket and the Test series against India had been limited to one bouncer per over, meant that our batsmen were just not equipped to handle the Australian fire power either physically or mentally.

I spoke out against the experimental rule at the time and was glad when the Test and County Cricket Board decided the experiment should be abandoned from the start of the 1984 season in our own domestic first-class game.

That may sound strange coming from a batsman, especially one who has no particular desire to have his features reorganised by a missile hurled in his direction at upwards of eighty miles an hour.

Yet I firmly believe that the experimental rule England tried to persuade the rest of the cricketing world to follow, in order to make fast bowling less intimidatory, at a time when Test attacks were putting more emphasis on fast bowling alone, increased rather than decreased our chances of being hit and, possibly, maimed for life.

I understand – even sympathise – with the reasons why England went it alone and then tried to make the rest of the world follow. But, when it became apparent that most other countries were not willing to co-operate, the experiment should have been dropped long before it was.

It was introduced in the late 1970s when some fast bowling was getting out of hand. Although some quickies have talked openly

14 'The most important thing to remember about cricket tours is that under no circumstances should we enjoy ourselves.' Ian Botham and Allan Lamb ditch *Daily Mirror* journalist, Chris Lander. Peter Smith (the author) stands back smiling, thankful it wasn't him this time.

15 And later

about wanting to spill blood, the vast majority have no desire to see a batsman being battered around the head and are genuinely concerned if they do hit one. But there have been the odd ones who seem to take a perverse delight in seeing batsmen jumping around the crease like demented puppets.

There have also been the odd ones who get carried away when they come across a wicket offering more bounce than they are used to. They simply lose control of themselves. There have been others who have had no control. They run up and let the ball go without knowing exactly where it is going. And, if they don't know, the poor batsman has no earthly chance.

With the Australian and West Indies attacks being built around their fast men, the incidence of short-pitched bowling has been on the increase. The 1984 West Indies side kept within the bounds of respectability for the most part, but even then Graeme Fowler remarked on his return to the dressing-room at the Oval 'I wonder whether anybody has told them they are supposed to be aiming at those three little pieces of wood sticking out of the ground.'

The trouble with the experimental one-bouncer rule inflicted on English batsmen was that we were being shielded from the crueller world outside our domestic game. To be able to cope with a good bouncer a batsman needs practice at playing against them, whether he adopts a policy of taking them on or leaving them completely alone. We were not getting that practice.

It showed clearly on that 1982/83 tour. I made no apologies for going on at some length about the issue, for it did have a vital bearing on the outcome of the Test series. It proved our downfall in so many ways.

When we got out playing at the short-pitched deliveries in the first innings in Brisbane in the second Test, it was decided we should adopt a safety-first approach, with the batsmen being advised to ignore them as far as they possibly could, certainly discount them as possible run-scoring opportunities.

But in my opinion this policy bred even more problems. We had so many short-pitched balls sent down against us that ignoring them meant that each over we received only one or two balls of a length full enough for scoring off. If they happened to be particularly good deliveries, it meant our run-scoring opportunities were cut to a bare minimum. That was no way to get back into a series once we had fallen behind.

Such an approach may have suited a Geoff Boycott or a Chris Tavare but it did not suit everybody. It did not suit me. I have always regarded shortish balls as potential run-scoring opportunities. Before any fast bowler gets the wrong idea, that doesn't mean I like receiving them any more than any other batsman does.

As a result of our general policy I believe we became a little too meek and submissive against the Australian pace attack, when I believe batsmen should be positive and assertive whenever possible.

Not until we were 2–0 down with two to play did we change our approach, just in time to win the Melbourne game. Not only had we become meek and submissive against the faster bowlers but we were playing off-spinner Bruce Yardley in the same fashion, allowing him to dictate terms. Handy as Yardley was during that series, he would not have rated in the top half-a-dozen off-spinners in county cricket.

I thought that he was being treated with too much respect, and said so at a team meeting just before the crucial Melbourne Test match. I probably said more than I intended.

Generally, on that tour, we held our serious pre-match team talk early in the evening of the night before the first day.

In Melbourne, after the usual pre-match net session on the day before the game, I found myself discussing tactics with Ian Botham over a beer or two during the afternoon. We decided we had to become more aggressive if the series was to be saved.

Our tongues loosened by a pint or two, we had plenty to say between us at that particular team meeting. I know a few eyebrows were raised by the strength of our feelings and the force of our arguments, but we carried the meeting. And nobody responded better the following day than Chris Tavare, with an innings which boosted our confidence and really set us on the path to victory, although we did not appreciate that aspect of it at the time.

Tav simply took Yardley apart during his 244 minutes at the crease for his 89 runs. I probably appreciated it more than anybody else because he made it easier for me during our 161 fourth-wicket partnership together. Yardley was never the same threat after the way Tav dealt with him that day.

It was an innings that would have staggered people in England who have watched Tav at the crease and written him off as nothing more than a stonewall crease-occupier. When he does decide to have a go he is a remarkably clean striker of the ball, as he has proved in the later stages of some of his one-day international performances.

Although our final first-innings total of 284 was disappointing after the 161 runs Tav and I had shared in 141 minutes, Tav had certainly wrecked Greg Chappell's initial attacking policy of putting us in when he won the toss.

Greg Chappell took the slip catches himself to remove our openers – Geoff Cook and 'Foxy' Fowler – against the new ball and then whipped on Yardley as first change. He was made to regret that decision.

There were some wide open spaces either side of the wicket on the huge oval-shaped Melbourne outfield, which had staged the 1956 Olympics, and Tav plonked the ball in many of them as he lifted Yardley over the inner ring of fielders.

Soon those spaces were occupied as Greg Chappell was forced to spread the field as the score – standing at 56 for three when I joined him – swept over the 150 mark. That opened up more safe avenues for runs when the faster bowlers returned without the usual cordon of close-in catchers.

We had taken the score to 217 when Tav fell, Yardley gaining some measure of revenge for the treatment he had received by leaping to his left in the gully to complete a two-handed catch when Tav attempted to cut a rising delivery from Jeff Thomson. He was just 11 short of a century he richly deserved. I admired him that day.

Unfortunately I was out soon afterwards and it was completely my own fault. Yardley got me too, only this time with his bowling when I got too far under an attempted pulled drive and was caught at deep wide mid-on. It was an undisciplined shot. I finished an innings of high promise with a century on a plate by apologising to Bob for the way I got out.

Aided by an all-too-familiar collapse, with the last seven wickets going down for the addition of only 67 runs, Yardley finished with a respectable four for 89, but his days of being a real menace to us were over.

The memory of the almost unbearable tension on the fifth and final morning of that Test before we sneaked it by just three runs when we had virtually given up hope, will always remain with me. It is the most memorable finish in which I have been involved.

They had sneaked a three-run first-innings lead. We replied with 294 in our second innings, when I again shared in the largest stand in the innings, putting on 83 for the fourth wicket with Graeme Fowler who suddenly found his best form after a miserable six weeks or so. Foxy had been handicapped by getting out in so many unlucky and unlikely ways, including being bowled when ducking under a full toss from Trevor Chappell in the match against New South Wales.

Sadly he was to finish that innings of 65 in pain after smashing a ball on to his foot – resulting in a chipped toe which was to put him out of the final Test. Derek Pringle and Bob Taylor also weighed in with useful contributions before our innings ended, leaving Australia needing 292 runs to win.

With plenty of time left it was a smaller target than we had hoped to present them with, but soon looked handsome enough when Flash Cowans produced some magical deliveries backed up by keen fielding, in which deputy wicketkeeper Ian Gould – fielding as substitute for Foxy – excelled in the covers. By the time last man Thomson walked out to join Allan Border on the fourth evening, Australia were still 74 runs short of their target.

It looked all over, but doubts began to creep into our minds as Thommo somehow survived. We lost count of the number of times he edged the ball through the slips, or over their heads, with nothing actually going to hand, as they reduced the target to 37 by the end of the day.

Our plan had been to concentrate on getting Thommo out, trying to get him to face as many deliveries as possible. When Border, who had been in miserable form during the first three Tests, was on strike, Bob spread out the field to give him the single. Quite often he over-indulged himself and took two instead by superb placement on Melbourne's large outfield.

Looking back we might have done better attacking Border as well, considering his lack of form, but Bob still kept the original plan in operation on the final morning as the pair inched Australia nearer and nearer home.

It reached the stage when only four were required, with Border – then on 62 – facing. We could not permit him one loose ball which he could send to the boundary. We could not permit him a single off the fifth or sixth balls to get the strike for the next over. Bob was bowling and produced what must have been his finest over of the tour. It was a maiden and there was nothing Border could do about it, so immaculate was Bob's line and length.

The agony increased with every ball bowled, but Bob's great over gave us another opening. With Thommo on strike and Botham bowling, we somehow sensed it would be the final over of the match which could have produced one of three results – a win for England, a win for Australia or even a tie.

One ball was enough. This time Thommo did get an edge that carried to second slip where Tav was fielding. It was a sharpish edge but straight forward. But the agony was still not over. Our hands started to go up in delight but the movement changed to one of absolute horror as Tav fumbled it and the ball went over his right shoulder.

In trying to catch it Tav had at least taken the pace off the ball. It seemed to hang in the air a long time – time enough for an alert Geoff Miller to run behind Tav from first slip to complete the catch for a staggering climax.

The effort left us completely drained mentally if not physically. I know callers to the dressing-room expected to witness scenes of absolute mayhem, with England cricketers dancing with delight, knocking back champagne as if Australia were going to run out of the stuff at any minute.

Instead, even an hour after the match had finished, they found the dressing-room more like a morgue – once it had been cleared of the immediate well-wishers. Most of us just sat around staring into space, hardly saying a word. Now and again one would make a move towards the shower and get changed. We were all too overcome to take it in properly. We made up for it that night.

Star of our show was undoubtedly Flash Cowans, who was given the new ball for the first time in the series at the start of the Australian second innings and responded magnificently with six for 77. Bob had spent considerable time with Flash before that match, building up his stamina, making him fitter, tightening his control.

Nothing had given him greater satisfaction in that match than dismissing Chappell twice – the first time for a duck off the first ball; I helped in that, taking the catch at deep mid-wicket off a hook. We had set Chappell up for that. In the second innings he had made only two when Gouldy dived full length at extra cover to complete a remarkable catch.

We were all delighted for him, and not just because Chappell was their main dangerman, having taken us for centuries in two of the three Tests. He had also taken Flash apart every time he had faced him, going back to the first match of the tour when we played Queensland in Brisbane. Flash deserved his revenge.

It was said that Chappell's onslaught in that Queensland match was a deliberate attempt by the Australian captain to dominate England's newest fast bowler right from the start, to knock the stuffing out of him before he could become a danger, especially as Flash was still very inexperienced and only twenty-one. I heard a different version.

For the previous six Australian seasons, starting with the formation of the Kerry Packer circus, Chappell has been taking on West Indian fast bowlers. The West Indies side were an important ingredient in the Packer circus. When peace was established between Packer and the Australian authorities and a deal worked out between them, the West Indies visited Australia for the following three years as well, either for a Test series and the tri-angular one-day tournament or just for the one-day internationals.

The 1982/83 season was going to be the first in Australia for seven seasons without a West Indian fast bowler in sight – according to the schedule. Chappell had said more than once he was looking forward to a more peaceful time.

It did not quite work out that way. Queensland's first Sheffield Shield match that season was against South Australia. And they had hired Joel Garner. He was the first bowler Chappell faced in that game. South Australia won it – and Garner won it for them.

Queensland's second match was against us. And the moment Chappell walked to the crease at the fall of the first wicket Flash was brought on to bowl against him. Greg decided there and then that Flash had to go. It was not a calculated assault with the Test series in mind, just a reaction at finding another West-Indian-born fast bowler racing towards him.

Flash was good news on the tour. He learned a lot. He also came in for a great deal of mickey-taking – just as I did. The lads were amused at finding a South-African-born player and a West-Indian-born player on the same tour party – both of us making our first tours as well.

It was the sort of situation which appealed to Botham in par-ticular. He was continually telling Flash such things as 'Don't forget you have to be up early each morning to clean Lamb's shoes and get his clothes laid out,' or 'When you share a room with Lamb you must get him tea in bed and fetch his breakfast', or 'When the ball goes past Lamb in the outfield, you must run and fetch it for him'. Flash took it all very well and maybe poking fun at apartheid in this way will help to show how absurd and horrific the system is.

That Melbourne victory made us believe that we could pull off another victory in the final Test at Sydney to save the series, especially as the Sydney wicket has favoured spin bowling and we had the better spinners in Miller, Eddie Hemmings and Vic Marks. It was not to be.

Two very vital decisions went against us which were to have a great effect on the outcome. We all thought John Dyson should have been given out run out off the sixth ball of the match when Bob scooped up a push by Kepler Wessels at the end of his follow-through and hurled down the wicket in one movement, but umpire Mel Johnson thought otherwise. Dyson went on to make 79, second highest scorer in Australia's first innings 314.

Then, in Australia's second innings when they were struggling at 90 for three, we were all convinced that Kim Hughes had been caught by Geoff Cook at short leg when he swept at a ball from Geoff Miller which appeared to bounce up off his toe. Hughes' wicket then would have put us right back in the game. He had made only 17 at the time but stayed to finish with 137. Our chance had gone.

It was sickening. Although we did suffer two heavy defeats and found it difficult to come to terms with their short bowling until it was really too late, there was not that much difference between the sides. I don't think there would have been any if Botham had managed to fire on just half his cylinders, but he never got going at all, either as a batsman or as a bowler. It was disappointing, because nobody tries harder out in the middle when playing for England, but his output never matched his input. He had a thin tour. It happens now and again. I know the feeling.

If we had been successful in holding on to the Ashes, I have often wondered how much credit we would have been given. Some people, particularly the Australians, would undoubtedly have made a big thing of the fact that both Terry Alderman and Dennis Lillee missed the last four Tests. Alderman following a damaged right shoulder, an injury incurred tackling a hooligan who raced on to the outfield during the first Test in Perth; Lillee through a knee operation during which splinters of bone were removed.

On the face of it they were Australia's two leading bowlers at the time. They could have been expected to play in all the five Tests. Yet, ironically, Australia's attack proved more hostile without them.

First Jeff Thomson and then Rodney Hogg were brought in to replace the pair – two express merchants to join Geoff Lawson. The extra pace they had over Lillee and Alderman made them tougher to deal with.

I think Lillee knew the end was near anyway, although he was still proving effective. He took three wickets in each innings of the Western Australia match against us and another three wickets in the first innings of the first Test on the same Perth ground – his home track. Each time he provided his side with a vital, early breakthrough.

It was the first time I faced him. Although he had lost that extra zip, it was still easy to see what a magnificent fast bowler he had been. Even the slower version was a handful. He had a great physique for a quickie, combined with a beautifully smooth and exciting run-up.

He always appeared capable of hitting the seam as well as making the ball swing. He had developed a nasty leg-cutter too. His control was generally immaculate and his change of pace so well disguised it was almost impossible for me to tell when he actually dug one in or when he produced his slower ball. But he was obviously not the threat he once was. Not that I minded.

He even apologised to me for not causing me more trouble than he actually did. It happened on a boat trip he organised. He tossed me a can of lager, sat down and said 'I used to bowl better than that.'

'You don't have to tell me that D.K.,' I replied. 'I saw you bowl on television when you were at your peak and I know your record. That's good enough for me. You're the best.'

I thought Hogg was the best of their bowlers on that tour. It has been suggested that he has proved a little suspect temperamentally throughout his career and needs things going for him to be

75

at his best. But when he does get it all together he seems to offer a little more than Lawson or Thommo.

He is genuinely quick with a good bouncer which goes through head high and not ballooning over the top. He bowls wicket to wicket and has the ability to move the ball both ways from a full length. I found I had to play at more deliveries from him than any of the others.

After Hogg, Thommo was the next in the problem stakes, particularly on a wicket offering him some bounce. He got that little bit extra every time and it was pretty uncomfortable playing balls from only just short of a length from around rib high and trying to keep them away from the close catchers stationed either side of the wicket.

He was still as unpredictable as ever with his slinging style with the ball coming from right behind his back. One ball would go down the leg side, the next wide down the off stump, the next over the head, so wide or so short there was no need to play them. But then, all of a sudden, he would get one absolutely right. It was quite a shock when it happened and you had to remain on full alert to deal with it.

Thommo bowled particularly well in the second innings of the second Test in Brisbane when taking five for 73. All five were in a row starting with David Gower, myself, Derek Randall, Foxy Fowler and Botham. The first three of us all fell to his shortish delivery which started the concern about our ability to play it.

Lawson also picked up five in that second innings to go with the six he had taken in the first innings. In pre-match interviews Lillee had nominated Lawson to take over from him as the 'king' of Australian fast bowlers and he went a long way in that match towards putting on the crown when given the new ball responsibility.

I did not think he was quite as awkward as the rest, yet he finished the series as leading wicket-taker. I suppose he was more consistently quick than the others and will be even more dangerous when he starts moving the ball away from – rather than into – the right-hander.

I would expect at least two of those three to be in England in 1985 plus Alderman, now happily recovered from that shoulder trouble. That is why I believe they will be a hard side to beat, even if it may be a strange-looking party with no Chappell, no Marsh and no Lillee.

With Carl Rackemann and John Maguire to provide the choice of back up, their attack will be useful in English conditions. Neither Rackemann nor Maguire possesses genuine pace but they are steady swing or seam bowlers of above medium pace. Maguire bowled a very good line against us for Queensland and in the one-day internationals. During 1984 the West Indies – who had just thrashed Australia 3–0 in the Caribbean – mentioned that Maguire had added an extra yard to his pace. It will be interesting to see what difference that has made if he is in the party.

The one player they will miss is Greg Chappell, especially as a batsman. He was such a polished, authoritative player who walked tall to the wicket, as though he knew he was going to take command. He usually did, his driving powerful and elegant, a model for any younger cricketer.

I have no idea how good he was against the shortish delivery early on in his career, but he was a little suspect against it when playing us in 1982/83. He did not fancy it, although he never ducked the issue. He was always prepared to have a go against it and we twice had him caught on the mid-wicket boundary hooking.

Two or three times early on in his innings, in the first Test in Perth, he might have been caught fending off short-pitched deliveries, but the chances did not go to hand. Once he had got over that however, there was no stopping him, anything loose but in reach fairly thumped to the boundary. He was most impressive.

His authority at the crease, his whole bearing helped him gain respect as a captain. He was not a man to stand any nonsense either, even if it came from Marsh or Lillee, two men who had grown up with him in the Australian side.

Greg would allow them to display an initial angry reaction when things did not go their way, but any attempt to prolong the antics would find Greg stepping in. He often made a point of showing the umpires, the crowd and the Australian cricketing authorities, too, that he had taken action.

Once, in the first Test in Perth, he held up the game and walked slowly but deliberately after Lillee, following him almost the entire way to the third man boundary to tell his fast bowler to calm down after Lillee had snatched his sun hat from the umpire, following his refusal to grant an appeal against a batsman earlier in the over. I was the batsman.

I was also the cause of his holding up the match when we played Queensland, because he wanted to clarify a point with an umpire. I had driven a six over long-off, a Queensland fielder actually catching the ball but falling over the boundary board in the act of taking the catch. He did well to hold on to the ball actually.

Rightly the umpire at the bowling end – inexperienced in first-class cricket – signalled a six but some Queensland players still thought I should have been given out caught. Greg calmed them down, but then held up play while he walked pointedly from his position at first slip to Test umpire Mel Johnson, who was standing at square leg, satisfying himself that the decision had been quite correct. I don't think such an action would have gone down well at Lord's, but the other Queensland players quit their moaning when they saw that Greg was satisfied.

Nobody challenged his authority as Test captain, which was one reason why the Australian selectors turned to him to lead the side in series at home, although he gave up touring towards the end of his career. With volatile characters like Marsh and Lillee in the side, they thought they needed Greg.

Whether it was a good thing for Australian cricket as a whole is doubtful. It meant that poor Kim Hughes, the stand-in captain for tours, never had any real chance of stamping his own personality on the leadership role.

He never gained the respect of Marsh, Lillee and some of the other older players and this was plainly evident when Kim was in charge of their last full tour here in 1981, and again in the 1983 World Cup.

Everybody knew that Kim would have to hand over to Greg again once the party returned to Australia. He was never able to indulge in any long-term planning, or set a pattern for himself. I doubt whether any other cricketing authority would have been so accommodating as to have one captain for home series and one for tours just to satisfy Chappell's wishes.

If Greg had been prepared to serve under Kim – as he did in the triangular one-day series at the end of that tour – it might have been better. Some of the senior players would still have looked to Greg for leadership and guidance in that situation, which would have been embarrassing for Kim, but Greg could have handled that smoothly with Australia's interests at heart, without appearing to undermine Kim's authority.

In individual strength the 1985 Australians may not be quite as strong as the side we played in 1982/83 or, indeed, the one Mike Brearley got the better of in that memorable 1981 summer when I was still qualifying. But they should be more of a team, a more complete unit. And, therefore, harder to beat.

There was one very strange experience for me in Australia in 1982/83. That was finding Kepler Wessels playing against me for Australia. Like me, he was born in South Africa. In fact we played in the same Western Province side together before he joined Kerry Packer, met – and married – an Australian girl and decided to make Australia his home.

After scoring a century for Queensland against us in the opening match of the tour in Brisbane, he was brought into the Australian team for his Test debut on the same ground for the second Test.

It added an extra dimension to the match, for we were each determined to do better than the other. He won that argument, scoring 162 in Australia's first innings when opening, whereas I made only 72 before Rod Marsh took off for that spectacular leg-side catch off a firm hit I thought would take me four runs nearer a century. But I think I can claim a little credit for Kepler's century – if credit is the right word.

He had changed a great deal since we had last played together and I was guilty of not taking that into consideration when I advised the line England should bowl to him. Even in his early days Kepler had a widish stance, but it was even more pronounced when I saw him again. I was to discover the reason later.

During his Western Province days he was prone to getting out in the gully region off a shortish delivery, bowled on or about the off stump, although being a very sound leg-side player. I advised England to bowl around his off stump, but Kepler had turned into a very sound player square on either side of the wicket against shortish deliveries. They were his most productive strokes as a result of his widening his stance. That, however, had made him more vulnerable against the ball pitched up around his leg stump and yet I had said it had been one of his strong points.

Ian Botham always likes to try and sort out a batsman with a short ball and needed no second invitation to do so against Kepler after what I had said. Ian grew more and more upset when Kepler smashed him with great distain to the boundary with square cuts or pulls.

As Kepler grew in confidence in his stay, which was to last just over seven and a half hours, the more Ian became frustrated, until he came over to me and said 'You know a few Afrikaans swear words, have a go at him.'

I thought up some juicy ones and indulged in a little sledging every time Kepler got within earshot, nobody else – least of all the umpires – having a clue what I was saying. For all they knew I could just have been passing the time of day.

Kepler knew all right, but it did not make the slightest difference. His expression never changed. For all the effect it had on his game I might just as well have been swearing in Afrikaans to a kangaroo.

Ian was even more upset that my efforts were going un-rewarded. He obviously did not think too much of me as a sledger. That night he had me teach him some Afrikaans swear words and insulting phrases which he put into operation himself the next morning. Again it did not make the slightest difference to Kepler's composure at the crease. There was one difference, however. This time the remarks did result in a gentle smile playing on his lips when Ian let go. He obviously realised what had happened and could see the amusing side of it. He could afford to. He had the last laugh with his century on debut.

To make things worse for me in my private battle inside the Test match, Kepler had the last laugh when I batted again. I had made 12 when Thommo bowled me a shortish delivery which I flicked off my hips. Although I did not catch the ball completely right I got enough bat on it for it to go for a certain four to the shortish boundary square of the wicket.

Or so I thought – until short square leg got in the way. It caught him right in the midriff before he could get his hands to it, doubled him up so quickly the ball was trapped in his body and I was on my way back. Who was the short square leg? None other than Kepler.

Despite the disappointments we suffered resultswise on that tour, it remained a surprisingly happy party, which was a tribute to manager Doug Insole as well as Bob Willis. It was a tribute, too, to those players who did not get much of a look in over the first two and a half months while the Test series was being played. Ian Gould, Vic Marks and Robin Jackman who had bowled against me in my first real taste of senior cricket all those years before in Bulawayo – were the three mainly concerned.

They were desperately disappointed not to make the side, yet it never showed in their approach. Throughout they remained keen, happy and willing to help in every way. They deserved the success they were to enjoy later when brought into the one-day side. I hope I can remain as chirpy if I ever find myself in the situation they were in.

CHAPTER 6

The attitudes that are changing the nature of the game

Australian wicketkeeper Rodney Marsh once called me 'a cheating South African.' He went further, from his position squatting some fifteen paces or so behind the wicket in a Test match, 'You're just like the rest of them. You're all the same' he shouted out, mixing in another couple of colourful words for added effect.

It happened when I had contributed 31 towards the 48 I was to make in the first Test against Australia in Perth on the 1982/83 tour – my first Test appearance against the Aussies. Dennis Lillee was bowling when I attempted to cut him and Marsh made a great song and dance about taking a catch behind the wicket.

The appeal was turned down by umpire Tony Crafter, much to the disgust of Marsh and the annoyance of Lillee who snatched his sun hat away from the umpire at the end of the over – the time Greg Chappell was forced to intercede and remonstrate with his fiery fast bowler.

The turning-down of the appeal for the catch was the reason for Marsh's outburst against me. The subject was raised again when Marsh eventually had an appeal against me upheld, this time diving forward to snatch an inside edge when I played forward against off-spinner Bruce Yardley, a smart piece of work.

Strangely, it was one time I did not find the remark particularly offensive, or get upset because somebody had stuck a South African label on me when I was trying to do my best for England. I knew it was nothing personal from Marshy. He was just letting off steam. He would have done the same if it had been a fellow Australian in a domestic Sheffield Shield match.

It was an example of what the Aussies call sledging. Making unkind and cutting remarks at the batsman, hoping to put him off his stroke, shake his confidence, make him feel uneasy so that he is not mentally tuned in to dealing properly with the next delivery that comes his way.

It didn't upset me, because I had grown up playing the game in the same way in South Africa, where it is up to you to give as good as you receive – better if you can manage it. I'd done my fair share of sledging in my time in the Currie Cup.

On that tour I was not alone among our batsmen in being the object of derisory comments, muttered through clenched teeth from the close in-fielders, or from Lillee, Thommo and Lawson, three fast bowlers not slow in uttering the odd oath and discussing your lack of batting skill when you have played and missed against them, or edged a ball just short of a fielder.

Everybody in the side came in for the treatment at some stage or another, particularly Derek Randall whenever he appeared in the sights of D. K. Lillee. 'Arkle' is a very twitchy person at the crease – and not only at the crease – always on the move twirling his bat, touching his hat or pads, walking around and talking to himself to aid his concentration.

Lillee just couldn't stand it. There was always plenty of verbal abuse going on between those two out in the middle, with Arkle giving nothing away in these exchanges. It was a form of tribute in a way because a bowler – or fielder – only resorted to these tactics when the batsman was successful, as Botham and I had done with Kepler Wessels in Brisbane.

That was how it was between Lillee and Randall. Although Lillee once told me that he always fancied getting Randall out quickly when the Nottinghamshire batsman opened for England or batted three, he never really liked bowling to him with an old ball when Randall batted down the order.

The exchanges between the two of them could be seen from the boundary edge, although they never became heated enough to force the umpires to step in. It was clear enough, however, to detect that something was going on with the arm-waving that was involved. Enough, possibly, to give the impression that it was war out there, with everybody hating everybody else. That is far from the truth.

The evening following my little incident with Marshy, the

England dressing-room door burst open after the day's play and in walked Lillee with a couple of trays loaded down with a delicious assortment of seafood. Lillee is a Perth man with a friend who owned a seafood restaurant. He had persuaded the friend to supply us with a treat.

Close behind Lillee was Marshy, Chappell and most other members of the Australian team, each one carrying two or three cans of lager to pass around the England team.

We all spent a pleasant and friendly hour together, eating and drinking, swopping stories, telling jokes, re-living past incidents. There was no reference to any of the remarks made in the sledging that had been going on. We were all pals drawn together by the game of cricket.

In fact there was never any real unpleasantness on that tour between the sides. Players who had toured Australia before all commented that the atmosphere was friendlier than it had been previously.

They played it hard in the middle – very hard, so did we, giving nothing away. Apart from the occasional sledging, very little is said between players from opposing sides once the cricket starts. There is no love lost actually on the field and the Ashes are very important to Australia – and England.

Once stumps are drawn, however, and you step over the boundary line towards the dressing-room area, you become friends again, ready to congratulate each other on outstanding personal performances.

I enjoyed those after-match dressing-room visits. It is tradition that the side batting visit the dressing-room of the side who have been in the field, one of those niceties in the game, recognising the fact that the fielding side are the more tired of the two, and in greater need of a rest.

It is something that happens only on tour these days, and only on tours of Australia and New Zealand. It doesn't happen to the same extent on tours to the West Indies although that situation has now improved, largely because of Ian Botham's special relationship with Viv Richards and Joel Garner.

Such get-togethers are rare in India and Pakistan, mainly because their players are non-drinkers for religious reasons, and also due to the security surrounding such matches these days. We travel by coach to the grounds out there, rather than in cars as we do elsewhere, and we are whisked away soon after the close of play with a heavily-armed police and army guard. It is a pity.

It doesn't happen in England, either, since the days of Test-match sponsorship by Cornhill Insurance. We are all grateful they came to the assistance of the game, as their help has enabled us to receive the financial rewards a sportsman should receive for representing his country in a professional game.

We are all conscious that we should do as much as we can to help them, and this we do by attending the room they have set aside in which they can entertain their guests after a day's play. If we can't all get there the captain makes sure we are represented by some members of the side every evening. Something had to go and it was those visits to the dressing-room. Cornhill always makes the opposing team welcome and we can mix there, but it is not the same when there are onlookers around.

The majority of what sledging there was in the 1982/83 series came from the Australian side. The England players are never supposed to indulge in these types of activities. A very strict disciplinary code has been imposed on us, especially in recent years.

Bob Willis, captain on the tour and the first captain I served under for England, is a strict disciplinarian where these matters are concerned, completely opposed to any of us showing any emotion on the field.

Any hint of it starting to break out and Bob would come down heavily on the player involved. He cared very much about the image of the game – the example we set – particularly where youngsters were concerned. All umpiring decisions had to be accepted without any display of dismay, shock or anger, until the player concerned was safely hidden away in the privacy of the dressing-room.

He set a perfect example himself and I had to admire him for that. When he became captain he made it clear to every media representative that he would never discuss umpires or any umpiring decision. He stuck faithfully to that policy even when Australian pressmen raised the question at almost every press conference.

I must confess I do not know how he managed to control himself so well on the field. By the very nature of their work fast bowlers seem to be fairly fiery characters with a very demanding job. It

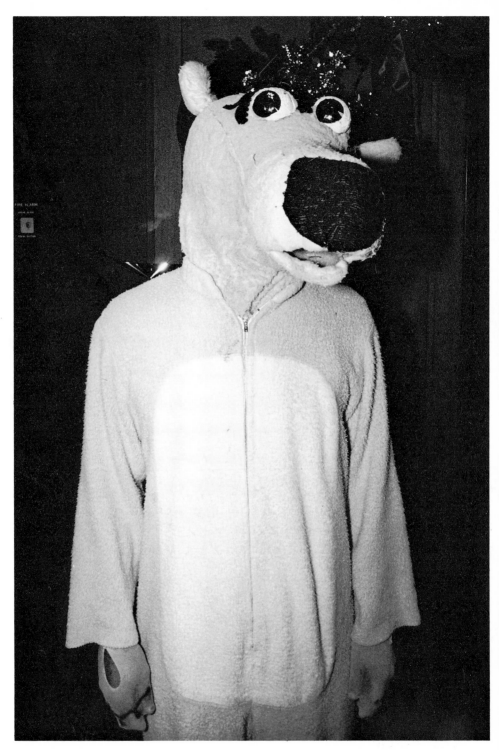

16   Allan Lamb deputising for the Pink Panther at the Players' Christmas Party;
December 1982.

takes a lot to remain fully in control of your passion when you have run miles in nearly a hundred degrees of heat on a placid wicket for nothing, then have an appeal unanswered when finally beating the batsman for a leg-before decision, or inducing a thin nick behind. Bob was unhappy about several decisions in Australia but it never showed on the field except for a brief flash of pain across his face.

Sometimes I believe we take our tight-lipped approach too far. I would not wish to do anything to spoil the image of the game. I recognise cricket has a fine tradition as a clean, wholesome sport, a reputation which helps it find sponsors of the highest calibre, who have turned their backs on football, because of the hooliganism involving so-called fans, and even on the part of the players.

Yet there should be some room and licence for a degree of emotion to be shown, as long as it does not get out of hand. There were times in Australia when we felt we were under a handicap in not being able to challenge anything. It is a tough game but we are in danger of looking a little soft. The opposition can take advantage of that situation.

The umpire is not always right. The standard of umpiring in England is higher than anywhere else in the world because English umpires have more experience of first-class games, yet even they will admit they make errors occasionally. They would not be human if they did not.

Throughout the rest of the world the standard is not so high. This applies in South Africa as well. Some umpires selected for Test matches or one-day internationals have had less than six first-class games behind them. I am sure they would appreciate it every now and again if their errors were pointed out to them, as long as it was handled in the right way. They would benefit.

I am concerned that our strict disciplinary code could be interpreted as meekness. In fact I am convinced it has been by some teams, and there is the danger that we could be trampled upon, as more and more importance is placed on victory in a commercial world, in which financial rewards are growing greater for winners.

The Australians play it very hard and that suited me. In fact I enjoyed the whole atmosphere and conditions, probably because they reminded me so much of the life I had led in South Africa and the conditions I had experienced in my cricketing upbringing.

The weather was similar with plenty of warm sun. The wicket conditions were about the same and the main cricketing centres are spread around the coast, with the sea never far away. I love seafood and Australia possesses the best in the world in my experience.

I got on with the Aussies, too, although some of the lads in the party got a little fed up with the macho image they tried to put across, of a hard-drinking, back-slapping, blunt, no-nonsense breed of men who are completely in charge.

Most of it is just a front. Argue back, shout them down, stand your ground and the aggression disappears. Underneath you will find normal human beings: generous ones too.

There was seldom a shortage of invitations to fill in the spare moments in between practice sessions or on the rest day of Test matches – invitations to beach parties, house parties, sight-seeing, boat trips, sea voyages, fishing or golf. You need diversions on a long tour, when it is essential to get away from cricket for a while and relax, especially on the whistle-stop tours undertaken these days, when you are forever going through airport terminals and moving from one hotel room on to another – which looks very much like it.

Not everybody feels the same, but I am one of these get-away-from-it-all types and there was some good fishing to be had in Australia. There is nothing better than standing on a river bank letting the mind empty, the frustrations and disappointments flow away with the water, draining the system and then recharging it for the next battle.

Australia is such a vast country. I had never really studied it before, stuck away as it is on the corner of a map. I can remember flying over it in the dark and the journey took hours. I remember Ian Botham, too, telling me to look out of the window and seeing the ground lit up for miles on end by bush fires destroying the outback.

Golf is a popular way for most of the players to relax on a free day and is an opportunity for mingling with the opposition. I don't think I am too popular on the golf courses with my partners. I can recall Jeff Thomson being more than disgusted when I partnered him once. I used to see him on the tee and then never come across him again until I caught up with him on the green. That was my fault. Although I can hit the ball a fair distance, the fairways are not places I visit very often.

Sydney was my favourite place. With the hotel in Melbourne being near the ground I saw little of that city. Brisbane was very friendly but deserted in the city centre until Thursday when the place came alive for three days. Perth was clean and beautifully situated on a curve of the Swan River; Adelaide neatly laid out in precision formation and quiet.

But Sydney had everything: magnificent beaches within fifteen minutes of the hotel or city centre; culture at the famed Opera House; fine back-street restaurants of every variety; delightful bays off the main harbour; jazz clubs that attract top-class entertainers; and the bridge, of course. It's amazing how you can kid newcomers that the bridge opens. Some of the party fell for it on that 1982/83 tour and received puzzled looks from the Australians when they asked for the opening times.

In some ways I think we were a little unfortunate in the timing of the tour, arriving in Brisbane only a fortnight after the Commonwealth Games had finished.

Australia had been particularly successful in the Games after having a few lean years internationally on the athletic track and in the swimming events. It resulted in a tremendous upsurge in national pride, the whole country – both new and old Australians – getting behind their sporting heroes. We were the victims.

The last day of the fourth Test in Melbourne was a typical example. Normally the last days of Test matches in England seem to be no-go affairs as far as the public here are concerned, even when a tight and tense situation offers the prospect of a thrilling, nerve-tingling finish.

When the last day started in Melbourne, the very first delivery could have been enough to have finished the game, yet there were 10,000 plus inside the vast concrete stadium. As word spread that Border and Thomson were inching Australia towards possible victory, even more flocked in, so that there were almost 20,000 – a full house on most England Test grounds – witnessing the actual death throes. Right to the end the Australian support was fanatical, which must have inspired the last-wicket pair.

It was the same everywhere in Australia, with the crowds going wild for the Aussies in the one-day games. In my experience it is

17 Another hard day's
work.

18 Allan Lamb
responds nobly to a no
ball from Richard Hadlee
in the second Test at
Headingley in July 1983.

the same everywhere else in the world when it comes to fanatical support for the home side – except in England, that is.

English crowds will rise to a perfectly executed cover-drive, a smart stop in the field, a tumbling catch. All receive a round of applause. They may even go a little overboard – by their conservative standards – when a six is struck, particularly if it is a hook-stroke against a fast bowler.

Occasionally, too, I heard the odd shout of 'Come on Bob' or 'Come on Ian' when Willis or Botham started to run in, especially at the start of a Test or if two batsmen had been in a long time and England needed a wicket rather desperately.

But I have never heard the whole-hearted roar of an English crowd getting behind their team, uplifting them by the noise and enthusiasm and passion. It is as if spectators in England are ashamed of being seen and heard offering fulsome support to their country and cricketers; frightened to raise any offered encourage-ment above a whisper in case their neighbours in the stands look at them askance, considering them idiots.

Maybe we have not given them too much to shout about. But, when things are not going too well is just the time when England should have the crowd right behind them, trying to give that lift which can make a hell of a difference. You like to know that somebody is on your side, rooting for you, instead of letting you play in silence, as if they, the England supporters, couldn't care less about the actual result, but only wish to see a good game of cricket.

It is ridiculous that, when their teams are playing in England, it is possible for Indian, West Indian and Pakistani, supporters to outshout the home crowd, even when they – the visitors – are outnumbered ten or fifteen to one. Even the sprinkling of Sri Lankan supporters – numbering no more than a couple of hundred – could be heard above the England spectators at Lord's in their one Test in 1984.

Mind you, they sell the game well in Australia since Packer and the Australian authorities got together, although the methods used would not go down too well at Lord's. They do, too, have the added advantage of the game being tied to a commercial television station, so it is in the interest of that station to stimulate interest, both to attract viewers and to make sure the grounds are as full as possible. The crowds are needed, for there is nothing more off-putting to a viewer than watching an event before empty terraces.

For days before a Test match the commercial channel is swamped with plugs for it, each one detailing how tickets can be bought and where. It would cost the TCCB a fortune to do the same in England.

The one-day internationals themselves – nicknamed 'the pyjama games' by the lads, with us all wearing coloured clothing and using white balls against black sight screens – became a really hard sell. The methods were successful; the crowds flocked in.

One outstanding memory is of a one-day qualifying match against Australia at Melbourne. More than 84,000 came to watch us: a record for one-day cricket. We managed to score 213 for five off our thirty-seven overs with rain having delayed the start, but Australia managed to beat us by five wickets.

The atmosphere was tremendous inside the stadium. It really was impressive. The stands do not look particularly high from the outside, but the actual playing area must be another twenty feet below the level of the ground outside. Looking up from the middle, the people at the back of the top deck appear little dots and we must look like ants to them. We felt like worker ants that day, as well, scurrying all around the outfield as Allan Border, John Dyson and David Hookes all scored 50 in passing our total inside thirty-five overs. It was another match we should not have lost.

The television adverts were crude in some ways. The insulting language was pretty strong, quoting so-called English gents saying that we would murder Australia and that Lillee and Marsh were 'over the hill'. Then Australian fans would be quoted on how their side would 'murder the Poms'. It was all designed to boost feelings; inflame passions.

The marketing company responsible for promoting the game in Australia made no secret of the fact that they were aiming the ads at people who were not cricket fans and did not understand cricket. This was deliberate.

They emphasised the result in a day aspect, trying to interest the 'new Australians' – the immigrant population from Greece, Italy, Spain, France and Turkey – who have no cricketing background but can understand that one side had to score more runs than the other.

It did result in a more unruly element creeping into the crowd.

We have experienced the same thing in our one-day competitions in England which have been attended by some soccer hooligans. In Australia it was the Australian Rules hooligan element who turned up. The marketing company argue that if they can attract them to one-day matches then some of them might find the game fascinating and be tempted to turn up at Test matches. 'They are our Test fans of the future. Not so much them, but their sons and daughters,' they claimed. It appears to be working.

As in England, the Australian authorities had trouble with the hard-drinking core, who sat in the hot sun all day swilling cans of lager. There was supposed to be a limit on how much each spectator could take into the ground and they were supposed to be able to buy only two cans at a time at the bars, the long queues to buy drinks making sure they could not get too many down them. But the fans always seemed to have enough.

There were some classic scraps on the famous Hill in Sydney, the smaller hill on the Brisbane ground and in the notorious Bay 13 area in the Melbourne ground, as the sun and beer mixed. At times the air seemed to be thick with beer cans as rival groups threw them at each other. Most of that was harmless fun. Unfortunately, now and again, a full can would be thrown. That was when the fights started.

Young women walking through the crowd were always a target for whistles and cat-calls. Some wags would take numbered boards with them, rating the looks of the women out of 10 in the way they mark ice skating, standing up with boards held out showing 9.9 or 9.7. Mind you, most of the girls seemed to love it, the way they dressed in revealing sweaters and the shortest of shorts.

Some people in authority even blamed the adverts, and the passions they aroused, for the disgraceful scenes in the first Test in Perth, when Alderman dislocated his right shoulder tackling a fan on the outfield, an injury which threatened his cricketing career.

It was doubly unfortunate that the twenty or so who climbed over the picket fence and advanced on the outfield towards the end of our first innings should be 'Poms' – either born in England or sons of English immigrants.

It had been evident for some time that trouble had been brewing on that Saturday, the second day of the game. There had been quite some movement in the crowd in the popular side, with groups wandering backwards and forwards. We could see it building up from the dressing-room area on the opposite side of the ground.

Then, all of a sudden, these twenty or so came over the top and raced towards the middle, holding up play. They were ignored until one teenager – walking away from the middle as the police moved in – clipped Terry Alderman around the back of his head as he attempted to snatch his sun hat. Terry saw red and chased him, finally bringing him down in a rugby tackle, but dislocating his shoulder at the same time, as other Australian players raced over.

As Terry lay stretched out on the ground, Greg Chappell led his team off. For a while Bob Willis and Bob Taylor – our last pair – stayed at the crease until they, too, started towards the dressing-room. They did not get that far. The umpires asked them if they would remain on the field in an effort to calm the crowd, and they did so, although it could not have been pleasant.

Terry was blamed for causing part of the trouble by the way he retaliated and chased the fan – something the Australians have done in the past. I can recall Rod Marsh pulling down a streaker at Edgbaston in 1981 and I also remember a picture of Greg Chappell catching another pitch-invader across the backside with his bat, a stroke worthy of a six if he had been connecting with a ball rather than a human being.

I don't blame Terry too much. He was walking away minding his own business when he received an unexpected blow on the back of the head. Chasing his assailant was an instinctive reaction. I don't blame the television adverts either. In some quarters there is a great deal of feeling between 'Poms' and Australians but social and economic pressures are the cause.

Poor policing was the main cause in my opinion, after it had been obvious for some time that a small section of the crowd had been growing more restless, insults and threats more menacing with every can of lager that went down. Long before the outbreak of violence more police could have been drafted in, especially as the Perth police headquarters were situated just outside the ground.

It was an ugly scene which I do not wish to see repeated. That, and the odd punch-ups at other grounds aside, I do wish English fans would wake up and copy the support the Australians gave their team. Even at home it can feel as though we are playing away.

CHAPTER 7

The guilty man

Controversy and yours truly appeared to walk side by side, fighting for England against the West Indies in 1984. In the space of five innings against them, right in the middle of the series, I emerged with three centuries to my credit. After two I found myself cast in the role of the guilty man.

Before Clive Lloyd started leading his side along the memorable road that was to result in the first white-washing of England for more than sixty years, I was in trouble with some of the game's critics but fortunately at that stage, not with England's selectors.

My poor winter form in New Zealand and Pakistan had some people doubting whether I deserved a chance in England's first Test side at Edgbaston. They had a point. In six Test matches on the winter tour I'd had nine trips to the crease but they had hardly been worthwhile. A total of 160 runs had come from them with a top score of 49.

I had not exactly won any admirers with my early season performances for Northants either, having failed to score a century before the first Test squad was chosen, but I had passed 50 on almost every visit to the wicket.

At least I had shown more consistency than anybody else who might have been challenging for the number five role in the England side. I had, in addition, made the highest score by an England player in the one-day International Texaco Trophy series that preceded the Tests, when making 79 in the first game at Old Trafford.

Most people had forgotten that performance in our 104 run defeat, and I don't blame them for it. It was rather overshadowed that day by Viv Richard's brilliant, undefeated 189 in the West

Indies' 272 total: the greatest one-day innings I have seen at that level.

It meant I went into the first Test at Edgbaston with something to prove, and failed to do myself justice. Only 15 runs in our first innings, two fewer in the second of our innings and 180-run defeat which set the pattern for the summer.

By the time the second Test at Lord's was due to get under way I was under even greater pressure. My last eleven Test innings had brought only 178 runs and I wondered myself whether I would make the squad.

I was very relieved to hear on the Sunday before the game that our new skipper, David Gower and the selectors had kept faith with me, although Peter May, chairman of selectors, warned publicly on the eve of the game that he would not tolerate any more individual failures.

'We have kept faith with several players. It is time they started repaying that faith,' he said. His message was aimed at up to half a dozen players in the side. I knew I was one of the targets.

Foxy Fowler was another batsman who had to take heed of May's warning and he responded with his second Test century, a very brave effort. The Lancashire left-hander is not everybody's idea of an opening batsman. They think he is a little too loose in his technique, but I have a lot of time for him. He lacks nothing in courage.

With Chris Broad, another left-hander, marking his Test debut with a half century, England opened with a century stand after Clive Lloyd had won the toss. Although he and Gower were to fall in successive overs from Malcolm Marshall, a platform had been established by the time I walked through the Lord's Long Room and out to the middle.

I did not make the most of it, making 23 before falling leg-before to Marshall to one which came back up the hill when I went out to resume my innings on the second morning. Disappointment overtook me. Both in my contribution and our final total of 286 after that century opening partnership. The mood soon changed when Ian Botham took the ball. He threatened to run through the West Indies all by himself in taking the first six wickets to fall.

This was Ian of old, making the ball swing in the cloudy conditions, teasing the batsmen with his change of pace so that only Viv Richards could live with him. By the time Ian had finished, with a little help from Bob Willis, the West Indies had been dismissed for 245 and we enjoyed a 41-run first innings lead. It was the only time in the series we were going to get ahead.

We were not to know it at the time. After the Edgbaston hammering we were ecstatic at finding ourselves in with a chance. That mood, however, was not to last too long.

By the time I walked to the wicket to join Foxy for the second time in the match, we had already lost Chris and David for 33 runs and Foxy went three runs later. It was vital I stayed in this time and I tailored my style to England's need.

We were only 124 clear when Mike Gatting was out on the fourth morning and I played second fiddle on another gloomy day, while Ian looked in the mood to take the West Indies apart as he scored 81 out of a 128-run fifth-wicket partnership before falling leg-before to Milton Small.

Paul Downton followed him and although Dusty Miller stayed with me while I completed my first Test century against the West Indies, taking almost five and a half hours, we were still struggling for the type of lead we wanted when he was out.

By then more than an hour had been lost to bad light, which meant the extra hour could be taken, taking the finish to seven. Long before six when Derek Pringle walked out to join me, the dark clouds were gathering again in one black mass behind the pavilion.

I knew we needed to get as many runs as possible that evening to put the match beyond the West Indies' reach, and to give ourselves a full last day in which to try and bowl them out. But I was also deeply conscious that we could not afford to be bowled out either, leaving the West Indies a last-day target of something in the region of four an over. That would have been easy for them to pace on a flattish track.

After almost six hours at the crease I was seeing the ball pretty well against off-spinner Robert Harper, and Eldine Baptiste, the slowest of the West Indies quickies, but I noticed that Pring was struggling as we started the final hour, particularly when facing Joel Garner who had replaced Baptiste at the Pavilion end.

Five minutes later and umpires David Evans and Barrie Meyer started to consult. In readiness for any bad-light offer coming our way I walked down the wicket to talk to Pring, noticing at the same time that Clive was calling up Marshall to take over from Harper, the new ball having been due half an hour earlier.

Pring was honest enough to admit straight away 'I'm having trouble picking the ball up.' It was not surprising in the conditions and having just come in. If he was struggling then, he would have no chance against Marshall and the new ball.

I had no hesitation in setting off for the dressing-room with my bat under my arm when the bad-light offer came, satisfied I had made the right decision as the senior batsman. There were a few boos and shouts from around the ground but I did not pay any particular attention.

Certainly I never anticipated the storm which was to follow, instead of congratulations over my century. Within minutes there were demands from the media for explanations, the walk-off being hotly criticised on radio, television and in the Press Box. The newspapers were full of it the next morning, with me taking the brunt of the criticism under such headlines as 'Incredible' and 'Disgrace'.

I was not alone in taking stick. David Gower came under fire for not being on England's balcony as the umpires consulted, ready to order me to stay in the middle if I had shown any sign of accepting the bad-light offer. Not being satisfied with having two cricket reporters at the match, one newspaper even sent a newsman to Lord's the following day to ask David exactly where he had been, and what exactly he had been doing, at the time the umpires consulted.

If David had been on the balcony I doubt whether it would have made any difference. I was so sure that the decision I took was right I never once looked in the direction of the England dressing-room. David would have needed a megaphone to get my attention and I don't think they have one handy at Lord's.

My decision was vindicated on the final day, when the West Indies were set 342 to win in five and a half hours, Pring and myself having fallen to the new ball first thing in the morning.

Such was Gordon Greenidge's authority in his astonishing double century backed by Larry Gomes' enjoyment of English conditions that they took the West Indies home by nine wickets with half an hour to spare. It was easy for them. It would have been a darned sight more easy if we had been bowled out on the fourth evening and they had had a full six hours to make the runs.

Something must have gone wrong at Headingley in the next

match. It did, to the extent that we lost the game by eight wickets this time, in what will go down as Marshall's match. But I scored a century again. For once I did not land in any hot water.

It was, in my opinion, the best century of the three; probably the best I have scored for England at the moment of writing. Everybody else in the side struggled, with the exception of Botham who made the second highest score of our 270 innings when reaching 45.

For some reason I found the going quite easy. I don't remember giving a chance and I reached three figures in the respectable time of 218 minutes, which is considered good going for Test matches. That century was completed in bad light, too. I had no sooner taken 10 runs off an over from Michael Holding to complete it when I was offered the light and accepted. Ironically Pring was at the wicket with me.

The West Indies' innings followed our pattern. They all struggled as well against the bowling of Paul Allott, who celebrated his England recall with a six for 61 return. It was high-class bowling.

The one he could not get was Gomes, who steered the West Indies into a 32-run lead, with the aid of a startling 59 from Holding, who swung at every ball, either missing completely or sending it to the boundary.

Larry was still four runs short of three figures when the ninth wicket fell, but was ordered to stay out there while Malcolm Marshall – who had been off the field all day nursing a fractured left thumb, an injury he incurred while making a stop in the field on the first day – hurriedly donned his cricketing gear and went out to bat one-handed. The move gave Larry his century.

Clive explained later that he was only joking in the dressing-room when he said to Malcolm 'You'd better get padded up.' He was surprised when Marshall immediately changed, because the doctors had advised him not to take any further part in the match.

If Clive was surprised, then we were astonished when Marshall walked out with the West Indies side at the start of our second innings, grabbed the new ball and proceeded to wreck us with his best Test return of seven for 57, paving the way for their eight-wicket victory.

Not surprisingly everybody was full of praise for Marshall's courage. The radio, television and newspapers were full of it. As far as I recall there was not one word of criticism directed at Clive

Lloyd for sending an injured man out to bat, purely to allow Gomes to reach his second century of the series.

Yet, a fortnight later in Manchester, David Gower was pilloried by some sections of the media for doing just that when I scored my third century in successive matches and I was accused of putting my own interests before that of the side. It's a strange world.

With Greenidge scoring another double century after Allott had taken three wickets in 15 balls, to present us with an early breakthrough, the West Indies managed to score exactly 500 when batting first. Marshall was missing from this match, but the West Indies found an ideal replacement in Winston Davis, called up from Glamorgan. He was second highest scorer with a career best of 77.

He was to have a far greater impact on the match when we batted, needing to score 301 to avoid being asked to follow on for the second time in the summer.

After Baptiste had broken the opening partnership of 90 when bowling Foxy Fowler, Davis came rushing in to break Paul Terry's left arm with a shortish ball that did not rise as much as Paul had expected on a poor wicket offering indifferent bounce.

It was the start of a disastrous slide as wickets tumbled cheaply. Again I was the only one who managed to stand firm, perhaps playing a few more airy-fairy strokes than I had at Headingley, but also finding the middle of the bat with great regularity. I was particularly pleased with my timing and driving towards the end of my innings.

I was still two runs short of my century when Joel Garner removed Pat Pocock and Norman Cowans with the second and sixth balls of an over. The figure we needed to avoid the follow-on was still 23 runs away.

Immediately Cowans' middle stump went I started walking back in the belief that our innings was over on 278. With Terry's left arm in plaster and hanging useless in a sling I did not believe there was any chance of his coming out to resume his innings. There had been no talk of it during the lunch break some forty-five minutes earlier.

Flash had not mentioned the possibility when he had walked to the wicket only three or four minutes earlier and the West Indies side plus the umpires had started to follow me off.

They were as taken aback as I was when David appeared on

the balcony and motioned me to stay in the middle. Some three minutes must have gone by before Paul emerged on the field, through a crowd of members, with a bat in his right hand, his plastered left arm and sling hidden by his sweater.

'What the hell is going on?' I asked him as I went to meet him. He told me he had come out so that I could complete my century. No mention was made of us trying to save the follow-on. I accepted that my century was the limit of our ambitions.

I accepted it, too, because Garner had come to the end of his over when dismissing Flash, which meant that Paul would not be facing a delivery. I did not think he should in his condition or even be asked to run quickly.

It was for that reason I took great care when facing the next over from Holding. I had been given an unexpected chance to complete my century and I carefully played the first five deliveries defensively.

The sixth was different. It was a little off line down the leg side. I got enough bat on it to nudge it wide of wicketkeeper Jeff Dujon for what I thought would be a safe single.

That was all I intended to take when I set off for the run, not because I wanted to keep the strike and try to save the follow on. That was not really on with Paul restricted as he was, for it would have meant me facing every ball. I took the single because I thought there was only one run in the stroke and it would have given me the strike for the next over in which I could search for the extra run for my century.

With my back to the ball I did not appreciate that Davis – fielding at long leg – had further to go for the ball than I imagined. When I reached the bowler's end and turned I saw it was still not in Davis' hand.

A second run was on with ease, especially as I was the one running to the danger end. I called for it to reach my century and immediately turned for the dressing-room once I had completed it, believing – for the second time – that our first innings was over 21 short of saving the follow-on.

I had taken half a dozen steps or so when I looked up and saw that David was still on the dressing-room balcony and was again motioning me to stay put. I believe Paul had also started to walk back.

I was more surprised this time than the first instance, for it meant that Paul had to face a delivery from Garner. I asked Paul what he thought and he answered bravely that he would have a go and see what happened. If I had thought that Paul had been sent out for any other reason than to accompany me to the century – like trying to avoid the follow-on – there was no way I would have taken the second run as I did.

As soon as I saw Paul try to play the first ball from Garner I knew there was no hope of his lasting. In order to protect his broken arm, he was forced to back away from the line of the ball which left him trying to swing the bat one-handed in the general direction of the ball.

He missed his first attempt by inches. I told him that whatever happened to the second ball, even if he missed it and it went straight through to Dujon, I would go for a run in order to get the strike. In the event there was no need. Garner realised he had only to pitch the ball up and bowl straight and it would be all over. He did just that.

David and I have never discussed the situation. I didn't see any point at the time I returned to the dressing-room, not realising the fuss that was going to be made of the apparent mix-up. I can only assume that David changed his mind as to Paul's mission from the time Paul agreed to go out there and the time I reached my century.

Before I had taken off my pads we had a message that most members in the Press Box were outraged by the goings on. Again radio and television were having a go. Either David was guilty of putting an individual before the needs of the team in sending Paul out just so that I could get a century or I was guilty of selfishness in being more concerned about my century in taking those two runs than protecting a handicapped Paul and seeing England over the follow-on figure.

It all created an unpleasant atmosphere and certainly did not help us in our task of trying to avoid defeat in that match. We had lost it by the end of the fourth evening when we were 120 for five.

That was four-nil down and the whitewash was staring us in the face then. It was duly completed at the Oval when they won by the handsome margin of 172 runs – through Clive Lloyd's captaincy and leadership.

He did not have to do too much himself to enable the West Indies to take the series 5–0. There are some people who will argue he has not proved himself a great Test captain, despite the tremendous success he has enjoyed leading the West Indies.

They will claim that, given the fast-bowling blasting power Lloyd had been able to call upon throughout all but the first couple of years of his captaincy reign, any other Test captain would have finished up with a similar record.

That is uncharitable and grossly unfair. There is no getting away from the fact that his fast bowlers have given him a decided advantage over every other side and maybe he has not had to think too hard on the tactical front from his position at first slip except, perhaps, whether to have three or four others with him.

But captaincy and the art of running a successful Test side is not only about tactics and cricketing knowledge. It is also about man management, getting the players to work for you, giving not just a hundred per cent but pulling out that little extra when danger threatens.

Above all, it is about getting individuals from differing backgrounds and lifestyles, habits and temperaments, working together as one solid unit, producing a team which functions as a whole instead of in bits and pieces.

That has been Clive's speciality. And that, I believe, is the reason why the West Indies were able to beat us 5–0 in the summer of 1984, producing the first whitewashing of an England side since Warwick Armstrong's Australians back in 1920–21.

Of course the West Indies wanted to thrash us in every game to show they are the top cricketing nation in the world. Of course it gave them extra pleasure because it gave a clear demonstration that, at this moment, black is better than white. Yes, that came into it. I don't blame them for that.

But, once the chance of a whitewash was on, after they had secured the series by winning the first three games and the weather showed no sign of breaking, they went remorselessly after that final 5–0 scoreline for one man – Clive.

The immediate after-match ceremonies at the Oval following the last Test were a shambles on the field owing to the fact that the West Indies were ten minutes late turning up and the crowd grew restless waiting for a sight of their heroes.

That was all down to Clive. Long before that Oval Test had finished he knew the players were going after the whitewash, not to enhance the West Indies cricketing reputation, but as an extra for him on his farewell to England as a Test captain. He was so overcome at the end of the victory that he locked the dressing-room door so that he could have a few moments alone with his team, before bedlam broke out, in which to thank each and every one of them personally.

Of course he has been the envy of every other Test captain as they have gazed out at him standing at first slip, legs wide apart, hands folded contentedly across his chest, looking out at the destruction before him from behind those thick-rimmed spectacles under his sun hat without an apparent care – except to decide when the time was right to bring back Marshall, Holding or Garner for another burst.

He very seldom has to worry about the timing of his declarations. When batting first he just lets the West Indies innings go on and on whether it has taken two or three days, knowing he has the fire power to knock the other side out twice in the time left. Two and a half days of West Indies batting usually means a 500 plus total and a very groggy opposition in no condition to offer stiff resistance.

When he has been forced to bowl first – or has done so at his own choosing – the formula has been the same again. Dismiss the opposition cheaply, build another mammoth innings and then let the quickies loose once more.

But there has also been more to Clive than these basically simple tactics. He has been in charge of three different sides now, each one raised to a position where they have been regarded as undisputed world champions at the one-day and five-day games. Even their surprising hiccough against India in the final of the 1983 World Cup at Lord's has not changed that ranking.

That has been achieved by superb planning on the part of Clive and his fellow West Indies selectors; achieved by the care Clive has taken of his players, especially in choosing the right moment to bring a newcomer into the side. It has been achieved because of the respect – even love – the players under him have shown for him.

Their admiration for Clive came through clearly in a number of chats I've had with Viv Richards over the years. Clive is like a god to the rest of the players. A father figure who cares for their every want and whim yet is never soft with any of them.

None of them wants to offend him or step out of line with him and that is true even of the senior players. He works them hard in the nets. There is no shirking. Last summer, when one of his senior bowlers had thought he had done enough practice and complained he was feeling a little tired, Clive said softly 'get on with it.' There was no arguing, no feeling of resentment. The bowler went on bowling until Clive was satisfied.

As a fast-bowling unit they simply have everything, a relentless attack hunting in fours which is at you all the time. The only respite from sheer pace and hostility came when Eldine Baptiste was introduced into the attack, yet he bowled such a good line and length you could not afford to relax for a moment.

Marshall is undoubtedly the key. He is known as the fastest bowler in the world and tries to live up to that reputation. He is also the meanest of the four; not in terms of giving fewer runs away but in his willingness to bounce you whenever he feels like it, and as often as he can without the umpire stepping in with an intimidation warning.

He can get a little bit carried away and pitch it short when the wicket conditions demand that he should pitch it up and allow the movement off the seam at his extreme pace to do the work.

Still his record speaks for itself. If he could steady himself a little more as a batsman, he could become one of the world's best all-rounders, in the Richard Hadlee mould.

He forms a good opening bowling partnership with Joel Garner because of their vastly differing styles as well as their difference in pace. Marshall's bouncer is probably more awkward than Joel's because it is more of a skidding variety, which catches you by surprise.

You know what to expect when Joel pitches it short. Bringing the ball down from his great height – his hand must be over nine foot in the air at the moment he releases the ball – it is bound to rise up, forcing you to play him from around your upper chest or just under the chin.

Marshall can also get the ball up that high from even a fuller length than Joel, yet his arm must be a good foot lower when he lets the ball go. That is why his bouncer is such a danger. Not many go over the head. You are constantly being forced to take evasive action.

What he hasn't got so far is Joel's yorker, which really is a beauty and must have brought him many of his wickets. It's at you before you really spot it, especially when you have been playing most of his deliveries from around your ribs. When he gets you, that big round face breaks into a beaming smile, the deep furrows on his brow smoothing away as the chuckles of delight flow. He really is a gentle giant.

For back up they have Michael Holding, once the sheer-speed star of their attack, a graceful animal whose feet barely seem to touch the ground as he races in like a quarter-miler on his long run. The umpires say that he is so perfectly tuned they seldom hear him approaching, but know when he is nearing the wicket by the whites of the batman's eyes. That's why we, in the England dressing-room, have christened him 'Whispering Death'.

Wear and tear have taken their toll on his legs so that he now operates off a shortened run, his action in delivery so smooth he has lost little in pace but probably gained more in his accuracy and control – not that it ever was much off line.

Just for a short three-over spell in the final Test at the Oval we saw a brief glimpse of the Holding of yesterday, when a West Indian fan – curse him – encouraged Holding to try his old full length run for a while. It happened in our second innings and brought him three wickets.

Chris Broad was the first to sample it, suddenly surprised by one that Holding made lift off a length with the extra zip his long run had given him. Chris could only fend the ball off to gully.

David Gower, whom I have seen have time to spare playing deliveries from a bowling machine switched on at 100 miles an hour, was next caught leg-before when beaten by sheer pace. I followed three balls later, scooped up by Desmond Haynes at forward short leg when I thought I had played the ball past him for a safe single.

Holding is a real gent, too, and – like Viv and Clive – fiercely proud of his Caribbean background. We came across him playing for Tasmania on the 1982/83 tour and were extremely grateful for his generosity and understanding when we played a one-day match on a pig of a wicket in Launceston. It was a brute, so bad that Tasmania made only 112 off the forty-two overs they faced, having as much trouble surviving as they did making runs.

Then it was our turn and we knew we were in trouble when, in Holding's second over, Geoff Cook got one that jumped off a length. He was fortunate in getting his bat to it.

Poor Derek Randall had no such luck in the third over from Holding when he replaced Geoff. It was another full-length delivery which rose up and there was nothing that Arkle could do to get out of the way. With his rather square stance with full face looking down the wicket, he was more vulnerable too.

He saw the ball rearing for his face, but it got up so quickly there was no time to get his bat up or even take evasive action. It caught him just below his nose, making a nasty mess of his mouth, an injury which put him out of the famous Melbourne Test a week later, as well as preventing him from enjoying his Christmas dinner.

It was not the sight I wanted to see when I passed him being led off on my way to the wicket.

Holding immediately sensed the danger. Instead of revelling in the conditions as some fast bowlers would have done, he immediately cut down his run, his pace on his approach to the wicket, the force of his delivery, and pitched every ball well up for the remainder of his spell. It was a gentlemanly gesture we all appreciated. Serious as Derek's injury was, there could have been a couple more even nastier if Holding had persisted in bowling short.

So much has been made of the West Indies fast-bowling strength that the threat of their batsmen is often overlooked – even with Viv Richards in the side. Now there is a batsman who has got more than his fair share of everything – including confidence which sometimes brings about his early downfall.

Anybody who saw his 189 in the first one-day international at Old Trafford in 1984 – either in the flesh or on television – will never forget it. Sheer batting murder and mayhem all the more remarkable in being built from a precarious West Indies position of 98 for six before it really got started. Neil Foster told me afterwards: 'No matter where I bowled to him he hit it.'

His genius that day was not so much in the power and per-fection of his strokes but in the way he was able to score at such an astonishing rate, yet remain so in control of a last-wicket partnership with Holding that realised 106 runs. Of the 88 deliveries sent down during that partnership Viv engineered it so that he faced 61 of them in adding another 93 runs to his total, exposing Holding to only 27. That was remarkable.

When he scored an unbeaten 84 in the third one-day game and

19 'It wasn't that funny.' Allan Lamb stands his ground while Dujon and Bairstow fall about laughing. Texaco One Day International at Old Trafford, 31 May 1984.

followed with 117 off 154 balls in the first Test at Edgbaston, we all feared we were in for another long summer of leather-gathering, but – fortunately – he then began to dry up. His last five innings produced only 69 runs, as we learned not to feed him so wantonly on the leg side at the start of his innings. I think, too, he became a little too over-confident after his magnificent start. Arrogance, some would call it, but that is something I have not detected in him.

Unfortunately for us Gordon Greenidge opened out at the very moment Viv started to dry up and he is not a bad deputy to have around. Gordon is very much a man of moods. If he feels it is going to be his day, then watch out. If he feels it is not, then he will grind it out with the best of them. We saw both moods during the series.

At Lord's on the final day, when they were chasing 342 to win in five and a half hours, Gordon obviously felt it was his day. He made a mockery of the target, helped by some admittedly loose bowling.

There was no hint of the havoc to follow when he first went in, he and Desmond Haynes taking 10 gentle runs off the first eight overs we bowled. Then Gordon thumped a couple of drives in one over against Ian Botham and he was away. There was no stopping him then. He can be as savage as Richards in that mood and proved it with his unbeaten 214 made off 244 deliveries.

His next double centuy at Old Trafford, two Tests later, was an entirely different affair, although the end product was the same in presenting the West Indies with victory. That 223 occupied just over nine and a half hours and 425 balls, yet such was his watchfulness and all-round control that I doubt whether he was beaten more than a dozen times in that period. It was an extraordinary display of concentration.

Their strength, however, was in always having somebody to rescue every given situation. They always appeared to bat with a freedom that suggested they knew somebody would come up trumps.

There was unsung hero Larry Gomes with 143 at Edgbaston and 104 at Headingley sandwiching an unbeaten 92 at Lord's. There was wicketkeeper Jeff Dujon with 101 at Old Trafford and, finally, Desmond Haynes rescuing an otherwise disappointing tour with a vital 125 at the Oval in the second innings. In fact the only batsman not to score a century was Clive Lloyd himself, when he wanted one so desperately on his final visit to England as a Test player.

If it wasn't a batsman it was a bowler, with Eldine Baptiste scoring 87 at Edgbaston and 44 at Lord's, Holding making 69 at Edgbaston and 59 at Headingley and then Davis weighing in with 77 at Old Trafford.

With bowlers like those around, who can bat to back up their fire power, I did wonder at one stage whether they needed any batsmen at all, or whether a team of fast bowlers would be enough, provided they were free to select from those who are now banned for life for taking part in a rebel tour of South Africa.

Perhaps a team of Michael Holding, Joel Garner, Malcolm Marshall, Colin Croft, Andy Roberts, Sylvester Clarke, Winston Davis, Eldine Baptiste, Franklyn Stephenson and Wayne Daniel with Jeff Dujon keeping wicket would be enough if they could ever settle the argument over the pair to use the new ball.

After the West Indies' picnic against us, we were supposed to have one of our own when we took on Sri Lanka in the first Test match they had played in this country. It really was a no-win situation as far as we were concerned.

If we had beaten them people would have said 'So what.' And we just could not afford to lose. I think Sri Lanka would have been happy with a draw before the match started. That is the way it turned out.

For once there was no pressure on me, which probably explains why I was able to relax and score a century, when most of the others struggled, when it came to our turn to bat. After my centuries against the West Indies I felt I had done enough to warrant a place on England's winter tour to India and that Peter May's warning about players needing to perform to book a tour place was not made in my direction.

Most of the others were not so fortunate. That applied to the bowlers as much as to the batsmen, although I had thought Paul Allott and Pat Pocock had also done enough against the West Indies to be sure of winter employment.

With the Sri Lankans themselves admitting they were short on class bowling, it was assumed the England batsmen could take them for as much as they wanted in any fashion they cared to choose. But that is easier said than done.

The lads knew that everybody expected them to score at least a half century and that put them under even greater pressure, especially after Sidath Wettimuny had made 190, Duleep Mendis had weighed in with an entertaining 111 and Arjuna Ranatunga scored 84. If they could do it, we were supposed to be able to go even better.

It meant that by the time we batted the price of failure was even higher, and explained why some of the lads adopted a more painstaking approach than they might otherwise have done. They could not risk getting out cheaply. In the end they fell between two stools. I was the lucky one in that respect.

I don't think, either, the English public gave the Sri Lankan batsmen enough credit for the ability they possess. I came across them a couple of times during the World Cup in 1983 – when they beat New Zealand – and thought then that three or four could become very good players with a little more experience against top-class bowling.

With the exception of Wettimuny who has always been a calm and patient player, ideal for the opening role, the others tended to be very excitable, losing their control when they started hitting out.

Right at the start of their mini-tour their manager Neil Chanmugam said the main purpose – apart from the Test – was to get his main stroke-makers to calm down a little, learn to hit the bad balls and defend against the good ones instead of attacking everything, as they have tended to do. By the time the Test came around they had proved themselves quick learners. I don't think run-scoring in good conditions is ever going to be their problem.

Drawing to them was a sad way to finish a summer most England players will want to push to the back of their minds. I will not. But I would willingly have swopped the centuries I made for a series victory against the West Indies for England's sake, desperately as I wanted to prove myself against the best team in the world and proud as I am of making them.

CHAPTER 8

The serious threat of New Zealand

David Gower was not the first England captain to get into trouble for permitting me to score a Test-match century. That honour fell to Bob Willis thirteen months earlier at the Oval, when I was also accused of putting the final nail in the coffin of Test cricket on a Sunday in this country.

I refute that charge, although I am not sorry to see the end of Sunday Test-match play, which had meant that we had to play five days straight off without a rest. The experiment was abandoned after that 1983 series against New Zealand.

Obviously I had no influence over the timing of Bob Willis' declaration of our second innings in that Oval Test match. My century did take a long time: some five hours forty-eight minutes to be exact, which is slow going for me. But the time taken was dictated entirely by the match situation.

I suppose what made it seem even worse in the eyes of the media and the public who allegedly turned their back on the game after my painstaking effort – only 5,000 turned up on the Sunday instead of 15,000 – was the fact that Chris Tavare had scored a century which was one hour and thirteen minutes faster!

Let me set the scene for the first Test of the four-match series. The first two days of the game, played in glorious weather, were dominated by Richard Hadlee enjoying the extra pace and bounce in the Oval wicket, both as a bowler and a batsman.

He wrecked our first innings with a magnificent display of accurate bowling combined with subtle variations of pace. He finished with six for 53 in our 209, with only Derek Randall able to stand up to his Nottinghamshire colleague in making an unbeaten 75 after a very sticky start.

Bob Willis proved just as hostile as Hadlee when his turn came to use the new ball. By the close of the first day New Zealand were 17 for three, soon to be 41 for five early the second morning. Hadlee changed all that when he joined Jeremy Coney in an 84-run partnership scored off only fifteen overs.

It was a frustrating stand for us and it boiled over at one point when left-arm spinner Phil Edmonds joined the attack and was warned for 'intimidatory bowling'.

As the bowler is approaching the wicket Hadlee has the habit of trying to kid and tease him by moving his back foot towards square leg as if making room to cut. If the bowler falls for it and bowls more leg-side in order to close down the space, Hadlee quickly switches across his wicket in order to pull or drive on the leg side.

He did this once against Phil, not a character who likes to be messed about. Phil's response was to bowl Hadlee a bouncer next ball, a harmless affair at his pace. Hadlee immediately walked down the wicket and prodded the pitch nearer the bowler's end than his own.

That upset Phil even more. He followed his first bouncer with a second. Under the one-bouncer-per-over rule operating in that series, umpire Dickie Bird had no alternative but to call it a 'no-ball' and then issue Phil with an intimidatory warning, as Hadlee again walked to within two or three feet of Edmonds at the end of his short follow-through and prodded the wicket once more. It was all rather silly.

By the time Hadlee had finished carving us around he had made 84 and New Zealand were within 13 runs of matching our first innings at the end of their turn. By the end of the day Tav and Foxy Fowler had turned that into a 159-run advantage when opening our second innings with a 146 partnership.

Saturday, another sunny day with a wicket getting easier all the time and more than 10,000 inside, was our bad day, although it had started so promisingly. Tav and Foxy completed their centuries, the first time for twenty-three years that both England openers had scored a century in the same innings. It was Foxy's first in a Test, Tav's second.

Unfortunately they were to get out within two runs of each other after England's double-century opening partnership. It happened as they were trying to play themselves in again immediately after lunch.

It was a double breakthrough which the New Zealanders in general and skipper Geoff Howarth – a shrewd tactician in the field – in particular, seized upon, with us 238 ahead, in attempting to put a stranglehold on our innings.

Jeremy Coney, Ewan Chatfield, John Bracewell and Lance Cairns may not be considered dangerous by Test-match standards. None are particularly fast but all are naggingly accurate medium-pacers with the ability to put the ball on the spot in a negative fashion.

They were not giving any runs away in trying to force us into errors. And we made them. David Gower edged a catch to slip, Botham and myself got in a terrible tangle over a single, which resulted in Ian being run out, and Randall edged another to slip.

With more than two days of the match to go – and the wicket not showing any sign of crumbling, – we were only 349 ahead with six wickets down when Phil Edmonds joined me at the wicket with an order from Willis 'stay until the close'.

I did just that. I did not turn my back on any safe scoring opportunity. At the same time I did not take the slightest risk and ignored some deliveries I would have gone for in different circumstances.

In doing what the captain ordered I spent the final three and a half hours of that glorious Saturday afternoon making only 43 runs. I was the villain again, on a day when England scored only 194 runs off the 98 overs New Zealand bowled.

One Sunday-paper cricket writer demanded my head the following day. The comments were even more bitter when Bob Willis delayed England's second innings declaration until after lunch on the Sunday and waved us in immediately I had reached three figures.

We were 459 ahead at the time. Most critics thought Bob should have declared at least half an hour before the lunch break, which would have allowed England's new-ball bowlers to have a double go at New Zealand – half an hour before lunch, a rest and then another burst immediately afterwards.

Perhaps, as it turned out with us winning by 189 runs, he might have declared earlier. But it is easy to talk with hindsight. At the time he was taking into consideration the ease of the wicket – even Hadlee could get nothing out of it on the third day – and juggling with the runs-against-overs formula, knowing there was still a long time to go. It needed only two New Zealand players to produce long innings and we could have been in trouble.

As it was we needed a stroke of luck to make our breakthrough when John Wright and Geoff Howarth got together in a third-wicket partnership producing 120 runs. They were beginning to take command when Wright pushed Vic Marks into the covers and started for a single. Tav rushed in quickly and his return beat Wright when he was correctly sent back by Howarth. He was slow in responding to Howarth's turn-down, explaining afterwards that he did not hear the shout because of his crash helmet.

Howarth was never the same after that upset, but New Zealand still needed fiddling out by spinners Marks and Edmonds before we won and Bob had the chance to defend both his declaration and my innings.

We sometimes get a little depressed in the dressing-room that people in this country do not seem to consider that a victory in itself is good enough. Not only do we have to win but we have to win in style. That is not always possible. In fact it is becoming harder still with India, Pakistan and New Zealand – teams England used to beat comfortably – now possessing half a dozen world-class players in their sides, instead of just one or two. Perhaps our recent victories – when we manage one – have been a little too workmanlike instead of inventive. Yet the overriding factor must be victory.

It was fortunate that we won that first Test at the Oval in 1983 with New Zealand winning the second at Headingley – their first in this country – on the back of some superb bowling by Cairns, plus high-scoring innings from Wright, Bruce Edgar and Hadlee yet again.

Thanks to Nick Cook's bowling – five wickets in the first innings and three in the second for a memorable debut when plucked out of a Leicestershire v Essex county match to replace the injured Edmonds at the last moment – we moved ahead in the series again at Lord's.

I had a disappointing match scoring 17 and 4. My only bad match of the three, as I had followed my century at the Oval with a 58 in England's first innings at Leeds. Yet, to my astonishment, I

20   Allan Lamb catches Evan Gray during the third Test at Lord's against New Zealand, August 1983.

was to learn that I faced the axe for the final game at Trent Bridge.

When the squad was announced on the Sunday prior to the match Surrey's left-arm fast bowler David 'Teddy' Thomas had been chosen instead of Neil Foster, who played at Lord's, and Derek Randall had been recalled after missing that game.

I learned later that the selectors had planned to use Thomas so that they could have a look at him in Test-match surroundings before they sat down to pick the winter tour party to New Zealand and Pakistan.

If he played it meant that one of the middle-order batsmen chosen had to go. With the match taking place at Trent Bridge they could not discard Randall again as the Notts fans would have caused uproar – with good reason. David Gower had to stay after scoring centuries in each of the last two Tests. It would have been unfair to drop Mike Gatting who had made his Test best score of 81 at Lord's. That left me facing the axe.

Bob Willis saved the day for me. On the eve of the game he insisted that I should be retained and the selectors finally agreed with him. In the end they did not drop a batsman as they had intended, but left out Thomas, although that meant we went into the game with only four front-line bowlers on a very good wicket.

I wasn't quite sure what it all meant as far as I was concerned. I did not know whether to think that I had done enough during the summer to have booked my tour place anyway, which was why they were thinking of leaving me out. That could have been one explanation.

On the other hand it could have meant they had some doubt about me in their minds. I reasoned that the only way to make sure of finding winter employment with England again was to put in a performance which would make it impossible for them to leave me out of the tour.

Once again I had Bob to thank for the opportunity. I managed only 22 in the first innings while Gower scored 72 followed by a century from Botham and an 83 from Randall which put us in command.

We totalled 420 and could have made New Zealand follow on when we dismissed them for 207 with Cook again taking five wickets. That left them 213 behind but Bob chose to bat again, showing a streak of ruthlessness.

With the wicket beginning to encourage the spinners he

21 Taking the rough with the smooth, Allan Lamb is given out caught Geoff Howarth off the bowling of John Bracewell in the fourth Test at Trent Bridge, August 1983.

reasoned he would be putting New Zealand back in the game with a chance if they should happen to score well a second time around, leaving us to bat last on a crumbling wicket. By batting again we would ensure a draw – barring a hideous collapse – which would be enough for us to take the series.

A collapse looked possible at one stage. I went in with the score 58 for two and started losing partners fairly regularly as I made my way to a century. I went on to make 137 not out, which still remains my Test best at the time of writing. Willis' plan worked perfectly with us winning by 165 runs.

I enjoyed that summer against New Zealand. In addition to the two Test centuries I had taken them for another when making 102 against them in the World Cup. Although Gower scored 12 more runs than I did in the series, I topped the England batting averages at 65.33. It was the first time I had done so.

So what went wrong six months later against the same New Zealand opposition when I could manage only 82 runs in the four innings I had in the three Test matches? I just don't know.

I know what went wrong for England. We were very close to winning the first Test in Wellington, still in with a chance on the last afternoon. We lost the second when we lost the toss in Christchurch on the worst Test wicket I have ever seen. Then, when we needed to win the final Test, we came across the flattest wicket you will find outside Faisalabad in Pakistan.

What went wrong for me I still haven't fathomed out, for I felt in good nick every time I went to the wicket – whatever the match. I do know it wasn't a surfeit of high living, which left us high on drinks and drugs, as has been alleged.

Certainly there were parties. The New Zealanders are a very generous and hospitable race. They are very conscious of the fact that, outside Auckland itself, there is very little to do in the evenings and hotel life does become a drag when one is living in them for three months at a time.

We were invited to many homes, the hosts inviting a few friends around as well. But there is one thing that should be made clear. The only latish nights around Test-match time were either on the eve of the rest day, when there was the whole of the next day to catch up on any lost sleep, or when the Test match was over.

I doubt whether, in the whole two months we were in New Zealand, there could have been more than half a dozen instances of a player having a drink in a hotel bar after midnight. Even then it was probably only one drink to repay his host of the evening, who would have driven him back to the hotel; and never when a Test had to be played the next day.

We were all stunned by the accusations that came flowing out of New Zealand the moment we had left the country – shocked by the half truths that were twisted and printed as hard facts.

I will quote a story I heard of the experience of one news journalist who was sent from England to investigate. The journalist tried every avenue possible to dig up dirt, but found nothing but praise for the way the players had conducted themselves and was told more than once that we had been good ambassadors.

That was not the story the journalist had been sent half way around the world to get. Fearing the displeasure of the editor if a story was sent back without any scandal the journalist included passages on drink and late nights without one shred of evidence on which to base them.

It is astonishing the lengths that some newspapers will go to in seeking a reason for an England cricketing defeat without accepting the one and only reason. We lost one Test match in New Zealand – and the series – because we were beaten by a team who adapted themselves to the conditions prevailing better than we did at the time.

It is amazing, too, how many people back in England seem to believe that we have no right to lose to countries like New Zealand, India and Pakistan because we once dismissed them with some ease. Have they no right to improve?

Take Martin Crowe as a prime example. He struggled in the Test-match series in England making only 163 runs in his eight innings yet he did enough outside the Tests for many coaches to mark him down as a fine prospect.

Not only a fine prospect at the age of twenty, as he then was, with a look of Greg Chappell about his driving – but also a quick learner. He learned from his mistakes over here and went back and eradicated many of them. He was two, three times the player when we next came across him playing in front of his home crowd and in familiar conditions.

Still people did not believe us back at home and I'm glad that Martin was able to prove that we were right by the high-class summer he had with Somerset in 1984. Once again he proved

22 Attack is the best means of attack:
Third Test at Lord's v. New Zealand, August 1983.

himself a quick learner, struggling in his early innings on the type of wickets we have to put up with for county matches but then adapting his game to enable him to overcome them in the end.

In 1984 Richard Hadlee proved himself the best all-rounder in the world today by achieving the double of 1,000 runs and 100 wickets, the first time the feat had been performed for seventeen years.

This was the same Martin Crowe and the same Richard Hadlee who had played against us in the Test series earlier that year. New Zealand had more going for them as well.

I have already mentioned Howarth's shrewdness as a tactical captain. Indeed many people rate him as the best there is around at this moment. In recent years the opening batting combination of John Wright and Bruce Edgar has been recognised as the next most reliable to the West Indian pairing of Gordon Greenidge and Desmond Haynes.

Jeff Crowe does not possess the flair of his younger brother. He is still a stickler at the crease, as is Coney. Cairns is unpredictable as a batsman, yet his big-hitting reputation is such that the crowd always buzzes when he walks to the crease. As a bowler he swings the ball more than any other, like a boomerang when conditions are in his favour.

Set against a background in which New Zealand cricket has taken off, beating every country who has visited them over the last six years, we knew it was not going to be easy when we first flew in.

Our attitude was also criticised, some of us taken to task because we gave the appearance of recovering our spirits after the Christchurch debacle faster than we should have done. We were accused of accepting defeat too easily.

Nobody would have made that comment if they had seen the faces in the England dressing-room during and immediately after our innings and 132-run defeat. We took it hard.

But that is no reason to mope for hours on end. Life still has to go on. David Gower took it hard being defeated in every match by the West Indies in 1984 but that did not stop him going out in the evening and enjoying a meal with friends, many of them engagements arranged days ahead. He said then that he found it essential to switch off every now and again and relax, otherwise the game would have got on top of him. And that would not have helped him or England.

Looking back on those two months and analysing them, we actually lost the series due to one man – Hadlee. He was the difference between the two sides at Christchurch, on the cracked wicket which had been causing concern before we arrived in the country.

The New Zealand officials were so worried about it they even considered taking the Test match away from Christchurch only a fortnight before the match was due to take place, but they received an assurance from the Canterbury authorities that everything would be all right on the day. Since our defeat, of course, they have removed Christchurch from their Test fixture list, insisting the wicket must be brought up to standard.

We had some bad luck before the Test match started. Graham Dilley was suffering from a thigh strain, which would not clear up and prevented him bowling properly. Then, even more tragically, Neil Foster had his small toe on his left foot broken in the nets in Dunedin only a week before the match.

I intend no disrespect to Tony 'Lester' Pigott of Sussex, who was plucked from a coaching engagement in Wellington and thrust into the Test as an emergency replacement, but the presence of Dilley and Foster could have made all the difference.

The next blow was in losing the toss, for it was obvious that the wicket was soon going to break up, so wide were the cracks and so loose the surface. When New Zealand batted first, we knew we had to get them out for less than 200 if we were to stand any chance.

That seemed well within our capabilities when they lost their first five wickets for 137 runs. We were even thinking that something around 160 would be their limit and the first day would belong to us after all.

Hadlee changed all that with a desperate innings of 99 made out of 144 added whilst he was at the crease, the majority in the company of Coney.

I say desperate innings because I don't think Hadlee expected to stay at the crease very long. He had watched the earlier New Zealand batsmen attempt to play properly and perish. If Hadlee's stay was going to be short before he met an unplayable ball, he was going to make it pay.

He has a wonderful eye and used it, driving and cutting. By the time he had arrived at the wicket, the edge had gone off our bowling. Pigott was suffering after giving everything in his first two spells, Flash Cowans was too short and Botham too wide. Even Bob Willis was forced to go down to his Sunday run in an effort to find control and try and put on the break. Hadlee never did receive an unplayable ball – he was reaching for a wide one when he edged a catch. We missed Foster's accuracy that afternoon.

By the time Hadlee was out, New Zealand had reached 281 and had made 307 when their innings finished, at least a 100 more than they should have done. We were thoroughly depressed and it got worse when Foxy Fowler was out in the final over of the day.

We were not helped by the weather on the second day. We arrived at the ground knowing we were up against it, but determined to put the first day's poor showing behind us. We had a fight on our hands, but were eager to get on with it. Instead we had to wait another four and a half hours before we were able to continue our innings. It was frustrating and it showed in the way we played.

Nobody can like hanging around and cricketers are no different. The mood is never the same after such a long hold up. The Christchurch ground isn't exactly built for comfort either. It's a rugby ground designed for people who are going to be there for two hours at the most and there was nothing to take away the boredom.

In the 90 minutes possible we lost a further six wickets, adding 47 runs, including mine for 11. By lunch on the third day we were following on, 225 runs behind. Soon after tea we had been bowled out a second time.

The match had lasted precisely two minutes over two days in actual playing time with Hadlee following his three wickets in our first innings with five in the second. Nothing had gone right for us from the moment that Foster had broken his toe a week earlier. That doesn't hide the fact that it was a miserable display.

It was doubly disappointing because everything had gone so well until that Foster injury, apart from our failure to win the first Test in Wellington. Everybody had made runs at some stage before that first Test and the fast bowlers were looking sharp, with Foster being the pick of them on his first tour.

We could have been only a fraction of an inch away from

winning that first Test too. That's all there could have been in it on the final morning, when a Nick Cook leg-before shout against Cairns was turned down just after the batsman had arrived at the crease. They were only 158 on at the time with just Ewan Chatfield to come and the wicket was a beauty. Instead another 118 runs were added before Cairns was finally given out. It was too late then.

Until late on the fourth day we had been in control. New Zealand had squandered the chance of first use of the wicket when bowled out for 219 and we gained a 244-run first-innings lead, thanks to a swashbuckling 138 from Botham and a spirited 164 from Randall, the pair sharing a 232 partnership in 201 minutes.

We had started making inroads into the New Zealand second innings when we came up against a stumbling block in the shape of Martin Crowe and his first Test century. Then it was Coney with *his* first in Tests and his first in any kind of cricket for seven years. Finally there was Cairns' highest Test score of 64, after surviving that confident leg-before appeal from Cook. That put the match out of reach.

With the Christchurch defeat following that left the final Test in Auckland to put matters right. It is the soundest Test wicket in New Zealand, offering nothing to the bowlers and very little to the batsmen either because of its lack of pace, and this despite the installation of an underground warm blanket to encourage the growth of grass on what is another famous New Zealand rugby field, Eden Park.

Our only real chance was to win the toss, bat first and make a huge first innings total in as quick a time possible, in the hope that they might crack mentally under the pressure. New Zealand won the toss, they totalled 496 for nine declared, with centuries by Wright, Jeff Crowe and wicketkeeper Ian Smith. And they took until the third afternoon – aided by 70 minutes lost at the start of the second day (although the conditions looked good enough to us) – to get that far. After all, they were not in a hurry.

We had no chance by then. It was a question of playing out time. I did make my highest Test score of the tour, a mere 49. And I was stuck on that score for an hour, mostly against the bowling of left-arm spinner Stephen Boock. I was determined to finish the series on a high note, yet just couldn't find a ball to get a single which might have got me going again towards a century. The new ball did me as soon as they took it with Cairns having me leg-before, a decision I did not take very well having played a long way forward to one that appeared to pitch outside the leg stump.

I did make one contribution before the New Zealand leg was over, scoring an undefeated 97 in the final one-day international, back on the same Auckland wicket. We had made sure of winning that mini-series – and extracting some measure of revenge for losing the Tests – by taking the first two games quite comfortably.

It was just as well for we lost the third, despite my contribution in our 209 total. Martin Crowe made sure I was a loser again with a century as New Zealand won with five overs to spare.

It was a tour most of us could have done without on our records, with the exception of Derek Randall. He was our star, with a century in the first Test, top score in the Christchurch defeat, another century in the third Test, plus a 70 to spark our victory in the first one-day international – plus his outstanding fielding.

Arkle really is a clown, a fidgety, laugh-a-minute funny man, although he is deadly serious when it comes to his cricket. Make no mistake about that. He is a worrier even, who goes down very quickly when he has failed, although he will shrug it off in public with that hysterical-sounding laugh of his.

When he has scored well, then there is little to contain him. You never know what he is going to do. Sometimes his room-mates suffer too.

He was sharing a room with Neil Foster when he made one of his vital contributions in New Zealand and left the ground happy. Neil was first back to the hotel room and was luxuriating in a hot bath when Arkle came bounding in and started making a cup of tea.

Fully dressed, he took a cup into Neil in the bath and then, still bubbling over with delight – promptly jumped into the bath himself – clothes and all. That's Arkle.

Another time in Adelaide, on the previous winter's trip, he was running a bath for himself when he heard a noise in the corridor outside his room. Dressed only in a towel, he stepped outside his room to see what the commotion was about. By then the corridor was empty. There was nobody around to help when his room door slammed shut with him on the outside with no key and the bath filling up rapidly. It had just started to flow over the top by the time he managed to summon help and get back inside.

He can be a nightmare to share a room with, for he is always making tea. He will always make some for you as well, which is nice – except when he fancies a cuppa in the middle of the night – and wakes you up with one too.

On the same tour he started an injury scare story when he was sharing a room with Flash Cowans in Brisbane. We were departing early one morning, which meant our bags had to be packed and sent down the night before. In his keenness to get organised Arkle packed early – and packed all Cowans' shoes as well. Poor Flash had to make the journey from Brisbane to Melbourne in bare feet, which caused travelling cricket writers to think he was hurt.

Although New Zealand produced one of the lowest points of my career, the tour also presented me with times that I do care to remember. The generosity of the people was outstanding, their willingness to organise things for us to do seemingly unending.

One of the most enjoyable times was the forty-eight hours we spent inland playing a one-day match against an Otago Invitation XI at Alexandra in the middle of South Island. We were so well looked after it was almost embarrassing. They had arranged everything to make us feel welcome.

The evening before the match I went out rabbit-shooting, chasing over the countryside in a Land Rover. It was rough but thoroughly enjoyable. Much smoother was the trip in a five-seater helicopter early the next morning. It whisked us up into the mountain range above Alexandra, offering us a view of the giant dam they are building, which will help turn the area into a vast fruit-growing range, and then on to a village where a splendid breakfast of bacon, eggs, mushrooms etc had been organised by a couple who have turned two old buildings into a superbly equipped restaurant.

The match itself attracted thousands, many of whom had driven several hundreds of miles from outlying areas to watch. The ground was in one of the most magnificent settings I have seen; surely one of the prettiest first-class grounds in the world.

The wicket and outfield is set in a natural bowl, surrounded by grassy slopes which climb fifteen feet or so providing natural terracing; the people at the top picnicking under sun umbrellas of every colour, which added a sparkle. The whole ground was then ringed by trees and, above them, you looked up at mountain ranges topped with snow, although it was over a hundred degrees out in the middle of the playing area.

Immediately the match was over, we were driven to Queenstown along a very picturesque route on a winding road through the mountains, with a river one side of the road racing along through narrow gorges. People still pan for gold in the area.

Queenstown itself is built on the side of a huge inland lake. It might easily have been in Switzerland, so beautiful was the scenery and it is the site of New Zealand's major ski resort.

With the co-operation of Mount Cooke Airlines, a wide range of activities were available to us on the one morning we had to spare. Ian Botham, myself and a few others chose to go shooting the rapids in a rubber dinghy. Another bumpy and hilarious ride.

Others elected to go on a trip down a river in a jet-powered boat. The boats are specially designed so that they can travel across water that is only two inches deep, reaching speeds of up to sixty miles an hour. The speciality of the driver is to get the boat up to near top speed and then put it into a spin which shoots up huge waves. The less adventurous, looking for a quieter time went up the mountainside in cable cars, whilst Bob Willis took things even steadier. He contented himself with a gentle trip around part of the lake in an ancient steamship 'S. S. Earnshaw'.

That was not quite the end. We flew from there to our next landing place in a small aircraft, which enabled us to go within a hundred feet of Mount Cooke itself as we twisted and turned between snow-covered peaks in the mountain range – such a contrast to flying across North Island where we witnessed the odd wisps of smoke coming from old volcanoes.

It was the most enjoyable forty-eight hours I've spent away from cricket on tour. It was a pity our next landing strip happened to be Christchurch with all that was waiting for us there.

CHAPTER 9

Qadired and trapped in Pakistan

Pakistan is a fascinating place to tour but there is something about playing against them (home and away) that disagrees violently with me.

I suspect it must be the bowling, for I have failed – and miserably – every time I have played against them in a Test match. After eleven attempts my highest score stands at 33 and I have also registered two successive ducks against them, fortunately not in the same match.

Australia apart, they are the only country who have denied me a century in my comparatively short Test career and I have never looked remotely like getting one against them, even when Imran Khan – the most complete fast bowler I have faced – has been missing from their attack.

The apprehension I felt when I flew into Karachi for the first time towards the end of February, 1984, following my New Zealand disappointments had nothing to do with the fear of failing against Pakistan a second time.

My South African birthplace was the cause of my worry, although I travel on a British passport. I was glad of the company of another South-African-born member of the England tour party in Hampshire's Chris Smith, who had made his Test debut the previous summer.

We both knew that the Pakistan players, the Pakistan Board of Control and Pakistan's President General Zia had no objection to our presence. We were not so sure about the students who were bent on causing trouble for the government.

For some time before our arrival there had been many clashes between students and troops. Casualties had been suffered on both sides, places burned and looted. The students may not have been too concerned about 'Kippy' Smith and myself but could have used our presence as an excuse for more anti-government demonstrations.

Neither of us needed to have worried. Everywhere the team went we were surrounded by armed troops equipped with walkie-talkie radios. Troops of every conceivable kind made their presence felt at all matches, mingling with the local police. Hundreds more were hidden within a mile of the grounds to prevent the kind of demonstrations that have ruined tours to Pakistan before.

It was my first exposure to this type of security, although the more seasoned travellers in the England party, such as Bob Willis, David Gower, Bob Taylor and Ian Botham have grown accustomed to it when visiting Pakistan, India and the West Indies representing their country in a Test match.

In Jamaica, on the last England tour in 1980–81 the team were assigned four heavily-armed personal bodyguards who travelled with them everywhere, revolvers at the ready, either in shoulder holsters when in plain clothes or strapped to the thigh, cowboy fashion, when in uniform. Naturally Botham challenged them to a shooting match on the police firing range. I think he lost that one.

The security in Pakistan was most impressive, certainly in numbers. Every time we left a hotel in our mini-buses we were greeted by truckloads of heavily-armed troops, who drew up in front and behind to escort us to the ground. Just how efficient the troops would have been in an emergency I don't know. One day I travelled to the ground in an army jeep. The driver wanted to give instructions to the driver of another escort wagon but the walkie-talkie would not work!

At the same time the army moved swiftly into action over an incident on the road journey from Lahore to Faisalabad, where we played the second Test. We travelled in convoy, two mini-buses for the team, another for the Press, two other trucks for the baggage and half a dozen jeeps, the backs of which were covered over to disguise the number of troops they were carrying.

They did not look as though they could carry more than six each, at the most, plus all their guns and ammunition. We found out differently two thirds into the journey, when one of the mini-buses broke down. It was well out into the country area, the road lined by trees and shrubs providing cover if anybody was intent on attacking us. Not that they would have had much chance. Within seconds of the convoy coming to a halt and a few shouted instructions, we were surrounded by troops equipped with rifles and machine-guns standing no more than two feet apart. It was baffling where they all came from.

Having that escort was handy. The journey would have taken hours otherwise, weaving in and out of the traffic. The rule of the road is quite simple in Pakistan. You simply give way if the opposing vehicle is bigger than yours, otherwise you are a goner. Much of the traffic on the road was larger than our mini-bus, which meant we would have suffered, but the armed escort cleared a path.

The only spot of bother we encountered was during the final one-day international in Karachi when a few evil-smelling, highly-coloured smoke bombs were let off on the terraces, causing the spectators to scatter. We wondered whether it might have been a signal for more serious rioting but nothing else happened.

All the same we could not help wondering what might have happened if a political demonstration had taken place and the police and army had been ordered to open fire to quell the rioters. Exposed to cross fire as we would have been in the middle, the thought was not very comforting. We did hear that some attempts were made to march on the ground in Karachi on the day General Zia was due to pay a visit, but the army turned the demonstrators away before they got near it. Wisely, perhaps, General Zia stayed away.

I might have become unnerved about the security aspect if I had thought seriously about it. Instead I needed all my wits about me to concentrate on staying fit and healthy during the month we were there. And I failed.

I don't think I have ever felt so rough as I did during the second Test in Faisalabad, when my head felt as though it were spinning, my throat was swollen and sore making eating virtually impossible, my chest heaved – and my stomach churned to keep pace with it. Playing cricket was the last thing I wanted to do at the time.

I am not putting my lack of health forward as an excuse for my lack of runs on the field – even though a lack of the runs was the thing I most wanted off it! Most other members of the side were in a similar state. Some were even worse, but were more successful on the field than I was.

Our dressing-room during that match had to be seen to be believed. Fortunately it was a largish one, allowing most of the sick to lie down in their varying states of discomfort. At one stage we were down to only three comparatively healthy players. One of those was Flash Cowans who was out of the match with a groin strain and another was Chris Tavare who had been left out.

We had already lost Ian Botham at that stage, because his left knee had finally given way under the strain of work and we had lost Bob Willis, who was flat on his back with chest and stomach problems, which were to force him out of cricket half way through the 1984 season at home, two months before he intended to retire.

It reached a stage when the batting order in our first innings – fortunately, in many respects, our only innings – was dictated by who was able to stand up reasonably steadily when a wicket fell. There was no way that Fowler could have opened when our innings started and he had to drop well down the order. Of the middle-order batsmen Randall was the fittest at the time and he went in at three when the first wicket fell.

By that stage Gower was flat on his back in the dressing-room and I was recovering slightly, which was the reason I went in ahead of him. The one saving grace was that the Faisalabad strip was the flattest, most bounceless wicket you could ever come across, which meant the weakest stood a chance of surviving at the crease. Not that it made much difference in my case.

Faisalabad was a distinctly unhealthy place, an industrial city where the full force of the sun was blotted out by layer after layer of dust filling the air. More dust was continually being thrown up by the oxen, camels and horses used as means of transporting the goods produced, never mind the lorries, buses, cars and scooters. I am convinced it was breathing in that dust-laden air which caused most of our troubles, rather than any food, for we were fed English-type meals every evening, specially brought over by road from Lahore a hundred and twenty miles away.

Much has been written in recent years about the spirit, the attitude and the approach of England players. Those who have cast doubt on our fighting qualities and willingness to defend the reputation of English cricket should have been in Faisalabad. I felt honoured to be a part of a group who simply refused to cave in when they had every excuse.

Result-wise we could not have been at a lower point, having lost the New Zealand series, suffered a defeat in the first Test in Karachi and the first one-day international in Lahore. We had lost our main match-winner Ian Botham and lost our captain and best fast bowler Bob Willis.

Yet, on wobbly legs, with upset stomachs and strained chests, the players rose up and got the better of a Pakistan side over-flowing with confidence. That took guts and character.

I have rarely seen Graham Dilley bowl faster than he did when Pakistan won the toss and batted first, yet he was suffering from damage to his nervous system which meant he could not feel his legs or the left side of his body. Immediately the match was over he was flown home to England for an operation which put him out of cricket for the entire 1984 summer. He deserved his five wickets in the game.

Despite his monumental effort and those of Foster, Cook and Marks – all suffering to varying degrees – Pakistan managed to make 449 for eight declared.

In the state we were in I don't think anybody would have been surprised if we had collapsed twice – on the field that is, for most of the batsmen were collapsing around the dressing-room. Yet we topped their score by 97 runs and even had them going in their second innings for a while before the game ended in a draw.

Although the batsmen did not feel like walking, let alone running, Kippy Smith and Mike Gatting scored 66 and 75 respectively as a makeshift opening pair sharing a partnership of 127. Randall chipped in with 65, Gower a wonderful 152, Fowler 57 and Marks with 83.

David Gower had taken over as captain in place of the sick Willis, his second time in charge of England. He is another who is very conscious of the image we should present, but I found he allowed us a little more latitude when we felt something was wrong on the field, although jumping in if it showed any sign of getting out of hand.

He was also prepared to ask the umpires for explanations over decisions, or make a point and this freer atmosphere helped us take a wicket in Pakistan's first innings when we did not look like getting one, although there was no question that the batsman was out.

Salim Malik was the player concerned, a brilliant young stroke-maker who looks like filling a middle-order batting place for Pakistan for some time to come. He had made 116, batting at number four, when he faced up to the last ball before lunch on the second day from Nick Cook.

He played forward defensively, misread the line and edged a catch to me standing at first slip. He had played with his bat away from his pads and there was no other way the ball could have reached me. I was not alone in being astonished when our appeal for a catch brought no other reaction from umpire Mahboob Shah than his taking off the bails for lunch.

As Malik walked off for the break I ran past him to reach the umpire about the same time as David, running in from mid-on. We pointed out it had been a straightforward slip catch and there was no question but that it had carried, for I took it knee high. He agreed to consult his colleague at square leg and only then did he give Malik out. The batsman was half-way back to the dressing-room by this time.

Mahboob later explained that he had not given a decision because he had been unsighted by Nick standing in the way at the end of his follow-through when bowling around the wicket, something Mahboob had warned him about two or three times previously. Yet he had made no move to consult his square-leg colleague in response to our appeal by the time David and I asked him to think again.

It was all done without any unseemly behaviour and Mahboob Shah was not offended in any way. Both David and I had hurried to him because it was the lunch interval and he had taken off the bails to signal the end of the session. There would have been no need for us to have done that if it had been the middle of an over. It was an instance when a little show of feeling had a reward.

The most encouraging aspect of our showing in Faisalabad was the way that Dilley and Foster responded when given first use of the new ball in the absence of Willis and Botham. As the only two quick bowlers in the team they knew we were relying on them and they did not let us down.

The same thing happened in the final Test in Lahore, except that it was Cowans and Foster this time, as a result of Dill being sent home for urgent medical attention. Again they responded.

Foster hit back with five wickets in Pakistan's first innings after we had been bowled out for 241, Fowler and Marks saving us with a 120-run sixth-wicket partnership with Vic finishing top scorer with 74.

Thanks to Fossie, Pakistan's lead was limited to 102 and we came very close to pulling off a staggering victory to even the series when making 344 in our second innings, with Gower contributing an unbeaten 173 and Vic passing 50 for the third successive Test innings.

We declared with nine wickets down, setting Pakistan 243 to win off the 59 overs remaining in the match. It was a gamble, with the wicket still playing well and Pakistan's side rich in stroke-makers, although their captain Zaheer Abbas was injured and could bat only with the aid of a runner. But David bravely risked going 2–0 down in an effort to square the series 1–1.

At one stage it looked as though we would lose, as openers Mohsin Khan, a most elegant player, and Shoaib Mohammad, the son of former Pakistan captain and hero Hanif, put on 173 before they were separated. There were fourteen overs left at the time with Pakistan needing another 70 runs. At five an over with all wickets intact, it looked like a formula for an England defeat.

It was at that stage that David brought back Flash for one last effort. And what an effort it proved to be. Undoubtedly it was his finest in Test cricket.

His Middlesex captain, Mike Gatting, seemed to have a hand in almost everything as well, helping in four dismissals as Pakistan lost six wickets for the addition of 26 runs before they gave up interest in victory and concentrated on denying us one. Five of those wickets were taken by Flash in four overs at a cost of 14 runs.

Gatting was at mid-on to take the first, catching Shoaib before running out Omar with a direct underarm hit from short mid-wicket in Flash's next over.

In his third over back Flash had Malik driving a catch to Gatting at short mid-wicket and his fourth over back proved even more dramatic. Gatting moved to square leg to catch Zaheer, Kippy Smith was at long-on to hold a skyer from Mohsin and Flash raced in again to dismiss Wasim Raja leg-before. Victory was so near.

It was the second time in the series that Pakistan panicked in sight of victory, for we had threatened to win the first Test in Karachi even when they started their second innings needing just 65. They had only three wickets to spare when they got them.

That wicket had bounce and turn. And Pakistan had that leg-spinning wizard Abdul Qadir to exploit it. He is marvellous to watch, except when you are at the crease facing him. He is even more fidgety when he bowls than Randall is at the crease. He is a highly-charged bundle who reacts as if he expects every ball to take a wicket, expresses disappointment when it fails and a spark of anger if he has an appeal turned down.

He won that first Test for them, destroying us once my former Northants colleague Sarfraz Nawaz had made the initial break-through each time, getting movement off the wicket none of our quicker bowlers could match.

With only two days to prepare for the Test after the widely differing conditions we had become accustomed to in New Zealand, we were bowled out for 182 in our first innings and 159 in our second with Pakistan making 277 in between.

David Gower was the only batsman to play Qadir with any confidence, while Ian Botham had limited success in his bid to blast the leg-spinner out of sight. The rest of us were bamboozled by his mixture of leg-spinner, googly and top-spinner. He got me three times in my five innings.

It was said that the best way to combat him if you could not pick him was to get as near to the pitch of the ball as possible and play every one as a googly – that is the ball turning into the right-handed batsman. If the delivery happened to be the leg-spinner instead – turning away from the bat – you hoped it would miss the edge altogether.

Everybody had their own methods. I tried to pick which way the ball was going to turn by watching it through the air rather than pick any subtle change in Qadir's action. I had limited success and it grew harder to pick the older the ball became. It doesn't stay very fresh on Pakistan's hard wickets. When that failed I had to resort to reading which way the ball was going once it had pitched. Whatever the method, a batsman must never go in half-hearted against him.

Gower coped with him wonderfully, occasionally finding his bat being drawn towards the ball as if attracted by a magnet when

23 Qadired – caught and bowled again in the third Test at Lahore in March,
1984.

it spun away from him, but generally curbing his natural in-clination to have a go. And Vic Marks was a revelation.

The way he played at Qadir in that first Test suggested Vic had never seen a leg-spinner in his life, yet he finished the series reeling off scores of 83, 74 and 55, more often than not going right on the back foot to read Qadir off the wicket and making the necessary late adjustment. It resulted in some strange jerky movements as Vic hurriedly thrust his bat this way and that at the last moment. It also resulted in success.

Vic also found the confidence to put force behind his strokes instead of merely defending and Qadir does not like that. Hit him two or three times and he quickly loses confidence in himself. He loses his line and length too. The difficulty is in being able to put bat on ball in the first place in order to hit him.

Qadir was not alone in causing consternation among batsmen in that first Test. Nick Cook did the same to Pakistan. He took six for 65 in their first innings and really scared them in the second when taking five for 18 as they struggled to make the 65 they required to win.

Perhaps we were a little fortunate in seeing so many familiar Pakistan names missing from their side. No Javed Miandad from Glamorgan, who was nursing concussion after being hit on the head by Dennis Lillee in a charity match. No Wasim Bari behind the wickets. And no Imran Khan who was still suffering from a stressed shin fracture.

I was not too unhappy that Imran was missing. I rate him as the most dangerous fast bowler I have faced. He came close to sweeping Pakistan to a series win against us in 1982, my first summer in the England side. He and his companion Mudassar Nazar, who always seems to have the Indian sign – or should it be Pakistan sign – over us.

At his fittest and best Imran is lethal, capable of running through any side. He can be as fast as Malcolm Marshall – and as nasty – when in the mood. And he possesses the added ability of being able to swing the ball both ways. Bowling at his extreme pace, that is a dangerous combination for any batsman to take on.

He is a very good batsman, too, with the ability to have played two or three places higher up the order than he did. He was good enough to earn a Test place on his batting alone, but it suffered because he was forced to take too much on as a fast bowler with Sarfraz not at his best due to injury problems.

Mudassar was a very deceptive medium-pacer. Pakistan regarded him little more than a change-bowler, although a useful performer in one-day cricket. At Lord's however that summer, he shook us all with six wickets in our second innings to hasten Pakistan to victory when we looked like holding out.

Both he and Imran swung the ball so much throughout that match, in conditions where our bowlers hardly got it to wobble, we even wondered whether they had found some ingredient to help make the ball swing.

We could not help but notice how the ball they used appeared to keep its shine longer than the one we used, although they are all taken out of the same box. We noticed, too, that the red stains on the whites of Mudassar, Imran, Sarfraz and Tahir – their four quickies – where they polished the ball appeared slightly different to the red stain on our whites. There was more of it too.

Before the end of the game we voiced our suspicions to the authorities and umpires and the balls were taken away for examination. Some years earlier it had been alleged that an Australian bowler had used a special substance rubbed into his trousers where he polished the ball to help it keep its shine longer and aid his swing.

The report on the balls used by Pakistan showed that no unusual substance had been used and Imran came up with a simple answer when he was asked about the suspicions at the end of the match.

He claimed it was because all Pakistan fast and medium-paced bowlers were more dedicated polishers of the ball than any others in the world because of the hard wicket conditions in Pakistan.

Over there the shine was removed very quickly, forcing them to really work on the ball even to make it last twenty overs. When they applied the same dedicated work on the balls in England, they kept the shine longer than English bowlers. He also pointed out that Pakistan bowlers also worked hard on developing the art of swing bowling because Pakistan wickets were, in general, useless for seam bowlers.

It was a tough series with nail-biting moments in all three matches. In the first Test at Edgbaston we were in danger of leaving them a simple target when we collapsed in our second innings, but Bob Taylor and Bob Willis came to our rescue with a

79-run last wicket partnership. Randall, too, played an important role with a century when opening, yet how he made it even he is not sure.

He could make nothing of Qadir so he took his life in his hands every time he faced the leg-spinner and attempted to belt him out of sight with some strange pulls-come-drives over the leg-side field. The method worked, but he might have been out a dozen times. The efforts of Randall, Willis and Taylor left a target well beyond Pakistan.

With the help of the weather at Lord's and the extraordinary patience of Chris Tavare we looked like saving the second Test when following on, Mohsin having boosted Pakistan's first innings to 428 for eight with exactly 200.

Mudassar had been allowed only four overs in our first innings but caused trouble immediately he came on in our second, removing Randall, myself – for a duck – and Gower at no cost. It was then that Tav dropped anchor to stave off an innings defeat with his half century, taking 236 balls and occupying 352 minutes, the second slowest on record. Nobody objected to his slow scoring that day. It was hailed as a masterpiece of defensive cricket.

He went on and on while Mudassar came back on the final day to snap three more wickets, lasting six hours 47 minutes in making his 82 and – with the help of bad-light stoppages – almost denying Pakistan time to make the runs they needed when our innings was finally over.

They had just eighteen overs left when they started off chasing their 76 runs, but they got them with 4.5 overs to spare, to win by ten wickets, only their second victory in England in twenty-three attempts.

That made it all square with the last Test match to come at Headingley, which produced another tension-packed climax – although time did not enter this one.

We were fairly evenly matched after the first innings, with Pakistan making 275 and England making 256 without any help from me, after I was dismissed for a duck again. When Pakistan were dismissed for 199 in their second innings, we were left re-quiring 219 to win with two days to spare.

The time did not matter but we were a little worried about the target against their attack. That mood had lifted by the fourth afternoon when Foxy Fowler, in his debut match, started producing a rich array of strokes. Although he lost Tav as a partner just after their century opening stand, Mike Gatting joined him and began confidently.

Victory looked on for that evening as they swept past 150 together but the light was beginning to fade as dark clouds gathered in the rain-producing area of the Headingley ground.

Twice they were offered the light but turned it down each time, both seeing the ball well and believing the end was near. It was undoubtedly the right decision at the time but it came close to undoing us.

It was all right as long as they stayed but when Mudassar came back to remove Foxy and Gatting was leg-before to Imran, the rest of us were struggling in the dark. I went for four, Gower for seven and Randall for a duck, five wickets having fallen for the addition of 21 runs with the victory target still 30 runs away.

By then it had got even darker and a fresh bad-light offer was accepted to take the match into the last morning. Even then the drama was not over. Ian Botham fell to the eleventh ball of the morning, leaving the tail exposed to Imran, but Vic Marks – making his Test debut – and the ever-dependable Bob Taylor took us home by three wickets. Phew!

They were a very temperamental touring party, much of it stemming from Imran who is not a man to keep silent if he thinks things are wrong. He spoke up and out. Unlike Bob Willis, he had made no vow of silence concerning the umpires and complained about decisions.

Maybe one or two did go against them during the complete tour, but I do not think they helped themselves by their antics in the field. Imran would openly show his displeasure when a decision went against him, while Qadir – in appealing for a catch by a close-in fielder or a leg-before decision – often jumped up and down in front of the umpires in an offensive way.

There was always a lot of chattering going on when they were in the field, most of it in their own language. Once at Lord's umpire Dickie Bird told them to quieten down, which provided an amusing story some weeks later.

He was telling the tale. 'There they were, all shouting and squabbling with each other in their own language. I thought to myself, this has got to stop. I said to them "gentlemen, gentlemen, calm down please, calm down." It was getting so loud and serious,' Dickie was saying earnestly, when he was interrupted by a member of his audience, who commented: 'If they were talking in their own language, how do you know they were arguing? They might have been asking each other where they were going to eat that night.'

'I hadn't thought of that,' said Dickie, bless him.

CHAPTER 10

Cricket in England – where has it gone wrong?

Bashing the overseas players has become a popular pastime in English cricket in recent seasons. The blame for many of England's current problems at a Test-match level has been heaped on our shoulders.

The current fast-bowling crisis has been attributed to the fact that the vast majority of county sides have imported fast bowlers from overseas, which has blocked a possible opening for a home-produced player.

The same complaint has been made over the importation of overseas batsmen. With the obvious exception of Yorkshire, every other county has employed one at some time or other to occupy a place in their middle-order batting – again filling a spot that could have gone to an Englishman.

Although I hold my hands up and admit I write with a biased pen, such charges, in my opinion, are complete and utter nonsense.

I do not believe there has been one English youngster – batsman or bowler – with outstanding promise who has been held back because of the presence of an overseas player in his county side.

Even if a county side has imported one of each type from overseas – as most have – that still leaves eight other places up for grabs, leaving aside the specialised wicketkeeping position. And nobody can tell me those eight other places are all filled by experts at their job. If they were England's selectors would have a hundred and twenty-eight players from which to select the Test side instead of the twenty or so who push for international recognition each summer.

There are too many mediocre players in county cricket for a promising youngster not to be given a chance to make the grade, if he has proved himself consistently in the second eleven. Where some county sides do make a mistake is in not backing promising youngsters enough, holding them back while they persist with a mediocre but more experienced older player, because he is more likely to keep his head in a crisis. That is a different story.

Surrey may have Sylvester Clarke, Somerset: Joel Garner, Hampshire: Malcolm Marshall, Leicestershire: Andy Roberts, but every one of those counties would still make room in their team for a young Trueman, Snow, Willis, Dilley or Lever if they had one on their books.

The same applies to batsmen, despite the presence of Viv Richards, Alvin Kallicharran, Javed Miandad, Clive Lloyd, Zaheer Abbas and others in English cricket. I can speak from personal knowledge on that score, on what has happened at Northants, my own county.

My presence on the Northants' staff has not hindered the progress of such players as Robin Boyd-Moss and Robert Bailey, two of the most promising prospects in the game at the moment, or others such as David Capel or Duncan Wild, two more who have a lot to offer.

England are going through a crisis in another department at the moment, a shortage of spin bowlers of true Test-match quality, which was demonstrated clearly when Surrey's Pat Pocock was recalled to play against the West Indies in 1984 after a seven-year absence – and at the age of thirty-seven. But nobody can blame the shortage of top-class English spinners on an influx of overseas spinners in the game because there has not been one.

The constant carping about the number of overseas players in English cricket and them blocking the openings for English youngsters may have done more harm than good. It would not surprise me if some youngsters have been put off taking up cricket as a career. My message to them is clear. Come and join us. There is always room for talent, the more the better.

No, the bringing of overseas players into the English game has brought about a number of benefits. With the grave shortage of English-born pace bowlers around how else would the likes of

David Gower, Graham Gooch, Graeme Fowler and others get the experience they need to try and cope against pace-dominated Test attacks but for the presence of Clarke, Marshall, Le Roux etc?

It has got to be the same for bowlers when taking on Richards, Greenidge, McEwan and company. They know they can't bowl rubbish at them or they will be murdered. They have to learn control, line and length. It must help them to become better bowlers, if they are capable of learning. If they are not, they are not much use to England anyway.

Putting the blame on overseas players is too easy. It disguises other faults with the system which are more responsible for the lack of progress of individual players who showed such outstanding talent when they were first introduced into the county side.

There are many other things that have got to be put right first, especially the wickets. Far too many of them used for normal county matches are not up to standard, making batting a lottery and even the most innocuous bowler a potential match-winner. That has to be wrong in these days when full covering is used.

Even at a Test level they seem to have deteriorated, not only in England but in many other places in the world as well. During his two years as England's captain, which involved him leading the side in twenty Tests, Bob Willis almost despaired of finding a wicket that did not start damp, the groundsmen watering them right until the final moments to make sure they did not crack up. Very few were fast and true, offering the degree of even bounce which all genuine bowlers need.

I blame the wickets as the greatest single factor for holding back players. Who can blame a sixteen-, seventeen- or eighteen-year-old aspiring fast bowler for wondering why he should have to put so much dedicated hard work into learning the arts of his trade, when he can watch any old Tom, Dick or Harry run through a county side bowling medium pace off a few strides and allowing a poor pitch surface to do his work for him?

Or who can blame a young batsman for wondering what he has let himself in for after years of learning to play properly, perhaps benefiting from the great work the National Coaching Association are doing, only to come across a wicket where one ball leaps up from a length and the next shoots through inches off the ground. It happens – and far too often.

We had trouble coping with the West Indies pace attack at the

Oval in 1984 because of the bounce in the Test wicket there. There was nothing wrong with the bounce. It was also even. The trouble, as David Gower pointed out, was in us having to adapt to what should have been regarded as a good cricketing wicket after the heaps we had been accustomed to in our everyday cricketing life around the country. He used a very apt and colourful adjective before the word heap, too.

Harry Brind, the Oval groundsman, has made a conscious effort to introduce more pace into the wickets there. Sometimes they have gone too far the other way with uneven bounce, such as happened with three or four used for county championship matches in 1984.

That was not the kind of wicket you want to find under your feet when facing Sylvester Clarke, the West-Indian-born fast bowler, who can be the most fearsome in the world when he puts his back into it, although both Boyd-Moss and Bailey stood up to him manfully that day considering their comparative inexperience.

Silvers is a huge man in every sense, with wide shoulders and powerful legs. He does not take a long run but possesses a very fast arm action which, combined with his strength, produces extreme pace. His bouncer is vicious.

Nobody fancies facing him on a quickish wicket and I heard a lovely story of a Warwickshire experience at the Oval a year or two back, when they were caught on a bouncy wicket with Silvers in full flow.

Every now and again he was producing a classic fast-bowling combination of a vicious bouncer, to have the batsman weaving and ducking on the back foot, followed by a yorker next ball – a combination which has brought him a number of victims over the seasons.

Those still waiting to bat could hardly bear to watch, yet their eyes were drawn to the middle in fascinated horror at what could be in store for them if Silvers was still bowling when their turn came. Among the fascinated watchers was Warwickshire manager David Brown, the former England fast bowler. He studied Silvers for a while and then announced to the assembled batsmen: 'I know what I would do if I had to go out and face him. I'd look down the wicket at him and ask if I could have the yorker first.'

Getting the wicket conditions right, so that batsmen are encouraged to play their strokes and bowlers of all kinds have to study their craft if they want to claim their victims, is the first priority before a more drastic change I would make to the Britannic Assurance County Championship system. I back the call Bob Willis and several counties have made to a switch to four-day matches.

To me that would make sense all round. It would produce a fairer championship if it had a programme of sixteen four-day games with each county playing the other once instead of the present twenty-four-match programme where you play some counties twice. That, surely, is cock-eyed.

In making this change English domestic cricket would only be falling in line with the main domestic competitions played in most other major cricketing countries. The Sheffield Shield in Australia is played over four days as is the Shell Shield tournament in the Caribbean.

Although the early stages of the Ranji Trophy in India are played over three days, the final stages when it becomes a knock-out competition are played over four days, as is the Duleep Trophy played between the zonal areas. In Pakistan the Quaid-E-Azam Trophy games are also played over four days.

Only in South Africa with the Currie Cup and in New Zealand for the Shell Trophy are the domestic first-class games confined to three days and I have been told there is a strong move in South Africa to switch to four.

It certainly makes sense from an international point of view, for the county championship would then become a proper training ground for Test cricketers, with the batsmen having an opportunity to build an innings and learn to play a long time, the basic requirement of a batsman in a Test match – as long as he remembers his run-scoring duty at the same time.

These days too many batsmen going in at four, five or six are denied the opportunity of building an innings. They have no chance, of course, in the limited-over game and in the championship they are usually looking for runs quickly in order to obtain their side an extra batting point or two before the first hundred overs runs out. In the second innings quick runs are often needed to set a declaration or to match a target that has been set.

It will be interesting, in the summer of 1985, to see the Australians playing a number of four-day matches against county sides over the weekends, a programme specifically asked for by the Australian authorities to allow their players to have better preparation for the five-day Test games.

The Test and County Cricket Board graciously accommodated them and I hope it will be the start of four-day championship cricket over here, although I doubt if that will come in until county clubs stop putting themselves first and think of the greater good of English cricket as a whole.

Some are against four-day championship cricket because of the reduced number of matches that would result. That, in turn, would stop the ones who play on several grounds organising cricketing weeks which are very lucrative, as local sponsors get involved booking tents on boundary edges, paying for lunches and match balls.

Others are against the idea because they fear it would upset members who could complain that they will be getting fewer matches to watch, for the money they pay, although I don't think that particular argument holds much water.

Sixteen four-day matches as against twenty-four three-day matches produces only four fewer home days cricket a summer. I can't believe members would complain about that if the quality of cricket they saw on the thirty-two days available was improved.

The argument over the loss of cricket weeks, which are enjoyed so much by Kent, Essex and Yorkshire in particular, has more to be said for it. I can understand, in a way, if they are against a switch, but they must also do what is best for the game as a whole.

Surely the first priority in this country is to make sure that the England side is the very best the country can produce, which means providing every aid possible to see that that side is equipped with the players trained to do the job required.

The success or otherwise of the England side must mirror the state of the game in this country. It is the England side that the public go to watch. It is the England side – and the image they create – which has a large influence on attracting sponsors to the game. The rest should flow from there. The greatest single source of income for county clubs comes from the Test and County Cricket Board when they share out the profits from the Cornhill Test sponsorship money, the Test gate receipts and the income from television and advertising associated with Test matches.

If England are unsuccessful for a long time and the income from Test matches starts to dry up because the side and the players in it are no longer as attractive as they once were, every county side suffers.

Instead of a sixteen match four-day championship providing fewer days cricket than members get now, it could be turned into an eighteen match four-day championship by making two of the Minor County sides first-class counties, a move that is being considered at this moment.

I am not so sure that is a good thing. With all the limited-over competitions plus the championship and the game against the touring side, there is enough cricket being played now. Perhaps a little too much for a very successful county, going well in all four tournaments.

Former players who remember the days when the championship consisted of twenty-eight or even thirty-two matches, will throw up their hands in horror at the suggestion that we may be playing too much cricket now. I know at least two selectors who will be dismayed.

I have lost count of the number of former players who think we have it easy these days, because we are not playing county championship cricket every day of the week as they did, although they did have their Sundays free. They notice we have several blank days in the middle of the season after rounds of the Benson and Hedges Cup or the NatWest Trophy.

That is very misleading. If a county cricketer played in every competitive match in the days when they played thirty-two championship games that would add up to ninety-six days cricket in the summer. Today's equivalent would play ninety-three days competitive cricket, if he were chosen for every match in the championship, John Player League plus the two knock-out competitions. And that is based on a county having a bad year in failing to reach the knock-out part of the Benson and Hedges and being knocked out of the NatWest in the first round.

There is one other aspect I am sure about too. It is far, far more demanding – both physically and mentally – playing a mixture of championship, one-day league and knock-out cricket than it was twenty-five years ago, when there was only the dear old championship to contend with.

It is those former players who had it easy. The present work load is quite sufficient and I would not like to see it increased. If anything it should be decreased slightly to make up for the strain of mixing one-day and championship cricket. Adding another couple of first-class counties would only increase that strain and add to the travelling problems which are bad enough. I know we do have an advantage there over players of twenty-five years or more ago, but even now we sometimes do not arrive at our hotel for the next match until after midnight. Especially during the 1984 summer with the ridiculous 117 overs a day minimum.

Through Test matches and one-day internationals I do not play as much cricket as a straightforward county player, but I felt done-in long before the 1984 summer had finished. I had been playing regular cricket since the start of the year, with only a three-week break between the end of the tour and the start of the new English season.

Rather than add two extra first-class counties, the game would probably be better served by chopping three or four and concentrating the better talent into fewer teams, which would make for better quality games.

This is where the two-division system, advocated by Ray Illingworth, does have some appeal. Understandably, the better players would want to stay in the top division, which would then become a super league, the best bowlers playing against the best batsmen producing better-equipped players for England.

At the same time I do not think the present framework of seventeen counties is too bad. I'd hate to lose some of the characters in the game which make it such a magnificent circuit to be playing in. Once in you have got friends for life. It's a slog. It can also be a barrel of laughs.

Not that I had any friends when I first arrived in Northampton, at the start of my four year apprenticeship, to prepare for the time England might want me. There were not too many laughs around the county either at that stage.

Alan Hodgson, a Geordie-born fast bowler, was to become my first close friend from among the team, and I shared a flat with him until I married in 1979 and my wife, Lindsay, came back with me. Several of the players were a little suspicious of me. They did not know much about me. I heard, later, that some of them did not think I could play.

There was not much help forthcoming at the time, either, because everybody else was pre-occupied by their own situation. It was a period of transition for Northants. Part of the playing force of the previous season had been broken off and not re-engaged – some pretty popular blokes among them too.

Two of the overseas stars had gone. India's superb left-arm spinner Bishen Bedi and Pakistan batting star Mushtaq Mohammad, who had led Northants to the Gillette Cup in 1976, had not been re-engaged. Neither had left-arm seamer John Dye, nor opening batsman Roy Virgin. Mushtaq had been a fixture in the Northants side for years, popular with the fans. I had taken his place. I had to prove my worth.

Northants had a new captain as well that summer in Jim Watts. He had been skipper before but left cricket to take up teaching. He had not played county cricket for two years when he was invited back to take charge. He found it difficult.

My first season proved to be a summer of toil and struggle for the county as a whole. We managed only two victories in the championship and finished bottom. We were not much better off in the John Player, failed to qualify from our group in the Benson and Hedges and lost the only match we played in the Gillette – hardly the start I had imagined.

Still, as they say, it could only get better after that – and it did. Geoff Cook, who took over the captaincy in 1981, and Wayne Larkins have formed one of the most successful opening partnerships in county cricket, easing the way for me to follow. In the middle Peter Willey was solidly dependable, the bowling getting stronger over the years to go with the advance the batting had made.

There was David Steele as well. One of the game's great characters with a good sense of humour, ready wit, down-to-earth approach and a reputation for short arms and long pockets which he enjoys. I knew him slightly in South Africa when he came to coach me as a schoolboy and he has been a part of my life ever since I have been in this country, even when he moved to Derbyshire for three years.

I always knew I was home and a new England season was about to dawn when I walked into the Northants dressing-room and saw a stale piece of chewing gum stuck to the wall just above the clothes peg 'Stan' Steele uses.

He deposits it there after his final home innings of one season so that it will be ready for his first home innings of the next. He swears he has changed the actual piece of gum now and again.

Stan, as he will readily admit, is careful with money. He doesn't believe in buying any new gear, for instance, until he has obtained every possible use out of his old stuff. We have grown accustomed to that, but even we thought he was taking it a bit too far a couple of seasons ago when playing Warwickshire at Edgbaston.

It had rained heavily overnight and the outfield not covered by the famous Edgbaston 'Brumbrella' covering, which protects nine tenths of the surface, was very soggy. When Stan ventured out he discovered his creased and battle-worn old boots were leaking. His solution was quick and simple. He nipped back into the dressing-room, found a couple of plastic bags and put them on over his socks to keep his feet dry. Smart thinking Stan.

Smarter still was his reaction during his time at Derbyshire when he was having run-up trouble delivering his slow left-arm spinners from around the wicket.

He was no-balled several times for over-stepping, his heel just going over the return crease by a fraction of an inch, but enough to be an illegal delivery. A slow bowler being no-balled for such an offence really is a cricketing crime.

Although Stan had adjusted his run up each time he was still transgressing. He solved his problem at the break by borrowing a pair of boots from fellow Derbyshire spinner Dallas Moir, who stands 6ft 8in. The boots were about three sizes larger than Stan normally wears but the extra inch in the length of the sole and heel meant that Stan cut the return crease line and bowled legally although his foot was still landing in exactly the same place as it was when he was bowling illegally – one mess Stan got out of.

Stan never seemed to have any cigarettes on him. In fact it has been said he existed on cigarettes supplied by Benson and Hedges or John Player at their sponsored matches and never smoked in the winter when they were not around to toss the odd packet into the dressing-room.

Alternatively, he used to borrow from the other smokers in the Northants dressing-room. We thought we had cured that habit when we stuffed a few caps down the end of a cigarette and left it sticking out temptingly from a packet we left in the dressing-room where Stan could see it easily during the lunch break. Sure enough Stan helped himself when he had finished his lunch – and carried on smoking as the caps went off in small explosions, sending tobacco flying around. He did look at it a little oddly.

The game is full of such characters and their exploits, providing a fund of stories for after-dinner speakers at cricket functions. The Essex team have always had a reputation for their humour and odd-ball activities, although they take the game very seriously.

Keith Pont is one of their funny men, once borrowing a bicycle to cycle across the outfield when Brian Taylor, their captain at the time, had him fielding at third man either end. I did the same when Eddie Barlow had me fielding in a similar position to both opening bowlers which meant a nearly two-hundred-yard trek in between overs. Not enjoyable on a hard Salisbury outfield under hot sun. I borrowed a bike from a spectator and rode across in between one over and the next, expecting Eddie to explode. Instead he saw the funny side of it.

CHAPTER 11

Assessing captaincy

The measure of David Gower as a man is that not once during the summer of 1984 did he complain about his lot. I spent a number of evenings with him, many after disastrous days on the field, yet he never bemoaned his fate.

I admired him for that. Even on the roughest days when, in his heart of hearts, he knew we were done for, he did not let the situation get him down, at least in front of the rest of us. He remained reasonably cheerful and optimistic.

That outlook was one ingredient needed towards making a good captain although whether David turns out to be the success the whole country must hope he will be, remains to be seen at the moment of writing.

It was too early to make a judgement one way or the other after the West Indies series. Certainly far too early to start writing him off and casting doubts, as some people tended to do.

Those of us who were with him in Pakistan when he took over after Bob Willis fell ill and finally returned home early, saw many other ingredients which all go to make up a successful leader once he had more experience.

He did a very good job out there rallying a sick and shell shocked side that could easily have been overwhelmed and torn apart when newspapers at home were printing every vicious rumour to come out of New Zealand.

We all recognised that the tour was likely to be Willis' last as captain with age creeping up on him. Towards the end of the New Zealand leg the speculation began to mount as to whether David would be his successor as seemed likely having been vice captain throughout Willis' reign. One or two in the party expressed doubt.

But those doubts were swept away once David assumed command and showed full authority. We were all able to relax a little more than under Bob who gets very wound up at Test match times through his desire to win.

David listened to advice from the senior players left and was always approachable, sometimes putting it into practice, sometimes working on schemes of his own. He was never afraid to ask for help which was another good sign. Too many I have known have gone their own way, stubbornly refusing to seek assistance or discuss possible alternative action with others in case it was seen as a sign of weakness.

During those two Test matches in Pakistan and the final one day international of the tour which we won with ease in Karachi, David also showed a spark of imagination, a touch of adventure and a willingness to gamble which was typical of a player who bats the way he does and is not often found among bowlers who are captains. By the very nature of the job they do in cricket which is a more defensive role in trying to keep down runs when wickets are not falling, bowlers tend to be a little more reserved and safety first as leaders, particularly the faster men.

David is not a demonstrative person. He gets upset by fools and idiotic remarks – as he did at Edgbaston in the first Test in 1984 when he stopped to challenge a spectator who was trying to be funny at his expense as he walked back through the members towards the dressing room – and getting out to poor deliveries. But he doesn't shout, scream and bawl.

It might just help him and the side if he did let rip just now and again instead of being so laid back to use a popular expression. He probably needs to show a little more of the killer instinct, the hard man approach and get the whole side to do the same. That should come with experience when he is a little more confident in what he is doing and the decisions he is taking.

The one great advantage he enjoyed in Pakistan was that he was able to lead from the front in scoring the 152 in the second Test in Faisalabad when he should have been in bed through ill health and his undefeated 176 in the second innings of the final Test in Lahore. Who could help give your all for a guy who had performed like that.

Those two performances eased a worry in the minds of many people about David as a captain. Bob Willis had expressed the fear two or three times that the burden of leadership might affect David's form just when he was proving himself a truly world class player. If anything, the leadership strengthened his resolve to make runs in Pakistan when he curbed some shots he might otherwise have attempted.

It was a pity his batting form did desert him against the West Indies which raised the question once again about whether England was sacrificing its greatest batting talent for the sake of finding a leader.

I am sure it was pure coincidence as Ian Botham always insisted it was in his case when he had his first taste of England captaincy against West Indies opposition in 1980, being doubly unfortunate in having to face them in two series in succession home and away.

The summer took a lot out of David and I did wonder whether he was as physically strong as he usually is after his experience in Pakistan combined with the attack of blood poisoning a few weeks later which resulted in him being rushed to hospital for a few days. I know that left him very weak and drained and he did not start playing cricket again until a week before the first one day international against the West Indies.

He would never raise that as an excuse but he did not get in the groundwork he would have liked to have done to take on an attack as strong as the one the West Indies hurled against him. After all that he went through during the summer and the whitewash at the hands of the West Indies, he must have been encouraged right at the end when Clive Lloyd voiced the opinion to the world that he thought England had made the right choice.

Until that series I had always found that David had responded to responsibility. He soon realised in Australia in 1982/83 that he would have to knuckle down as vice captain and take on the main responsibility for England's scoring especially with Ian Botham not showing any sign of being able to take the Australians apart as the whole country feared when he first arrived.

David was brilliant throughout that tour. He set the pattern in the first Test in Perth when a century looked certain as he scored 72 out of a 95 run second wicket partnership with Chris Tavare until a diving catch at square leg by John Dyson to hold a firm clip ended his stay.

He scored a century in the third Test in Adelaide and really went to town in the one day series when scoring three centuries. The best was undoubtedly his 158 out of our 267 for six against New Zealand in Brisbane. His third half century in that innings took only 29 balls during which he twice sent Hadlee over long leg for six with superbly timed pick-up shots off his legs.

He followed that by taking two centuries off the New Zealanders during the four match Test series in 1983 so, by the time the West Indies series arrived, he had proved England's most consistent batsman for almost a two year period. Not even Gower can win them all and keep going without some change in fortune.

I shall always be grateful to his predecessor Bob Willis for the support he always gave me during the two years in charge. The start of my England career coincided with his appointment as England captain so there will always be a strong bond between us.

Although I had set my heart on playing for England in 1982 once it had been pointed out to me it was possible, I did not expect to get an immediate call-up the moment I became available although the newspapers had been predicting my inclusion from the time it became obvious England were going to lose the 1981/82 series in India.

Bob must have been for me right from that moment. He stuck by me for the winter tour of Australia even when I had that dreadful time against Pakistan and, as I have already detailed, insisted on my presence in the final Test against New Zealand at Trent Bridge in 1983 when the selectors had earmarked me for the 12th man position.

I found Bob very good at getting people to work for him. He could always motivate me, the sight of him giving his all running in on those long, gangly legs of his for mile after mile which left him gasping for air as he strove for an England victory, was all the inspiration I needed.

He could grow tense and a little tetchy at Test match times, seemingly unable to relax without the aid of hypnotherapy. He plays hypnosis tapes on his cassette recorder made by a friend in Australia Arthur Jackson, the tapes discussing his problems and giving him confidence.

Bob would use them in the evenings mainly to help him wind down from the day and get to sleep at night. He is a very poor sleeper. During the 1982/83 Australian tour he introduced Chris Tavare to the tapes hoping they would help Chris relax at Test match times and unfreeze him at the wicket so that he could score as well as just survive. Whether Tav uses them today I do not know.

Considering the pressure he was under in being both England's one and only out and out quick bowler and captain I thought he did a good job. Having to bowl fast and lead was a handicap, probably asking too much of an international captain.

When he was actually bowling he poured all his concentration and effort into getting the ball down the other end as effectively as possible. In between overs during his spells he was too concerned in getting his strength back for his next six ball burst to be able to give his mind freely to what was going on.

At those times he relied on David and Ian to make the adjustments in the field as they thought fit which they did but anything major which might have cropped up was a problem because of the difficulty in communicating with someone who was often 100 yards away.

It was a great pity from his and England's viewpoint that Bob did not always get the fast bowling help from the other end he desperately needed to take the strain off his own shoulders. Considering that Graham Dilley made his Test debut in Australia in 1979, it was not often that Dilley and Willis teamed up as a fast bowling spearhead for one reason or another.

One or other of them seemed to be unfit. Willis had to come back from the West Indies in 1980/81 when Dilley was on that tour and kept going. Since then Dilley has been in and out either through loss of form or injury and we have not had the best out of him that we might have done.

The way that Dilley bowled in Faisalabad and Norman Cowans bowled in Lahore with Neil Foster in support suggested England could have a very impressive fast bowling combination in 1984 but that was wrecked by Dilley's injury received on tour which put him out of the whole summer.

I have gained the impression from talking to both Dilley and Cowans and listening to other people, that too much has been expected from them at times. Too many people – albeit with good intentions – have tried to offer them advice and change them leading to a confused picture.

Far too many people worry about whether they have their feet in the right place, the arms in the right place or they have not quite got a classical action and have tried to make them adjust, make them model fast bowlers in text book style. It is all right making

24   Posing on the Electron electronic scoreboard, a snip at £4 million.

those adjustments to an action when they are young but not when they are adult.

The first major essential for a fast bowler is basic speed as Dennis Lillee once told Dilley, getting the ball from one end of the pitch to the other as quickly as possible. It surely doesn't matter how ugly and ungainly the action. There have been some world class fast bowlers who offend coaching manuals but are still deadly dangerous, Mike Procter being one of them.

The refinements can be added later and gradually, not all in one go in the way that some people have tried to change both Dilley and Cowans. It has to be hoped that Dilley makes a complete recovery for he is still only 26 and Cowans is still some way off reaching his peak.

Finding people with the basic qualities of pace, strength and ball sense was the first priority of a scheme proposed towards the end of the 1984 summer by Ted Dexter and Bob Willis in their search for fast bowlers. They were not worried whether the individual concerned could actually bowl in a straight line at the time. They hoped to be able to teach that once the individuals satisfied them of the basic qualities. They were not searching for text book actions. Not all fast bowlers can be a Michael Holding or a Dennis Lillee.

It was a scheme that appealed to Bob after the setback he had received the previous summer. He was so concerned about the lack of fast bowling talent in the first-class game, so worried that one or two bowlers who looked likely prospects were not receiving the right kind of advice, he once asked the Test and County Cricket Board for permission to get ten or so together for a teach-in lasting a week or even a fortnight when he could pass on his knowledge. Unfortunately the scheme was turned down through lack of funds.

Some players, of course, just do not help themselves, seem quite satisfied with their lot at a county level without any will to make themselves better and play without any great show of enthusiasm. That is why it was so magical to have Pat 'Percy' Pocock back in the dressing room during the West Indies series. Even at thirty-seven he was still a great enthusiast, that fourth Test at Old Trafford might easily have been his first instead of his eighteenth gained some seventeen years after making his first appearance for England in the West Indies.

I was particularly glad to see him walk into the Old Trafford

25   Ian Botham

dressing-room on the day before the Test. 'Do you realise, Percy, that if you had not been recalled for this match then I would have been the old man of this side,' I told him when we reported for net practice. And I don't consider myself old at thirty.

After the first day of the game when the West Indies had recovered to 273 for five with Greenidge and Dujon scoring centuries and Percy had gone wicketless through two very tight and economical spells I can remember him muttering to himself as he changed 'I refuse to get depressed, I refuse to cry. I'm going to enjoy myself in this match and I'm going to walk out of this dressing-room smiling.' He thoroughly deserved the four wickets he took on the second day.

He was not so successful with the bat, failing to score in his first four innings back for England, which brought a certain amount of ribbing as well as a great deal of sympathy. It also explained, he said, why he carries a rather battered cricket suitcase around with him for all his cricketing gear rather than the normal regulation-sized 'coffin' used by almost every other player. 'It allows people to take the mickey out of my case rather than me or my batting,' he said.

Percy deserved a run for his effort in the first innings at the Oval when he went in as number three, acting as night watchman towards the end of the first day. He stayed around for 45 minutes on the second morning against their new ball attack and could not have been encouraged by seeing Graeme Fowler forced off injured when struck on the arm by Malcolm Marshall. It was Marshall who got him in the end as Percy attempted to avoid a bouncer only to edge a catch to slip. It was a nasty ball and not the first bouncer Percy had had to contend with.

His brave stay earned him a tribute from Paul Downton when he finally arrived back in the dressing-room. 'I must say Percy,' Paul commented 'that is the finest duck I have ever seen.'

He deserved a run that innings and should have got one in the second when facing Michael Holding. The actual drive was not particularly convincing but the ball found the middle of the bat and would normally have gone for one if not two. Instead Holding stuck out his right hand as he was following through and snatched a fine reflex catch out of the air. 'I don't mind getting out to a catch like that, even when I haven't scored, but not when I'm in the middle of a run glut,' muttered Percy sadly.

I was partnering him at Lord's against Sri Lanka when he finally got off the Test mark that summer, a single that Percy greeted as if he had just completed a century and a run which brought the entire England side out on to the dressing-room balcony to applaud. It showed how Percy, a non-stop talker, had fitted in so well with a group of players who had not even played for England when Percy was last in the side.

My century was still a couple of runs away when he walked out to join me at the fall of the eighth wicket. I knew he was desperate to get a run and I told him that I would play for him. 'I'll take all the strike for a while because just staying around in the middle will give you confidence. Just you tell me when you are ready,' I said.

For a couple of overs I did just that until I could sense that Percy was feeling at home. I took a single off a fifth ball of an over to inch a step nearer my century expecting Percy to block the sixth to allow me the strike. The field spread out a little to cut off runs and keep Percy under pressure, but he managed to squeeze the ball into a gap and came charging down the wicket. I wasn't quite expecting that but got home safely enough.

'Sorry about that,' said Percy later 'But when I saw there was a run in it I couldn't resist going for it.'

Two things have disappointed me about my England career up to the end of the 1984 summer. I am disappointed I have not shared in more big partnerships with David Gower and Ian Botham. With any other England batsman, come to that. And our semi-final defeat against India in the 1983 World Cup at Old Trafford.

Apart from the double century stand shared by Tavare and Fowler against New Zealand at the Oval in 1983 and another between Ian Botham and Derek Randall in Wellington on the New Zealand tour, I can't remember any other large stands.

It does seem strange that with the quality batsmen England possess, so many of our innings rely on just one batsman coming off, another making a major contribution and the rest filling in with bits and pieces.

In my two years we seem to have spent hours in various matches bowling at the same two batsmen sharing partnerships of 150 yet we very seldom produce a stand of that magnitude ourselves. Apart from my maiden Test century against India when I had Ian Botham as a partner for much of the time on his way to his

26   David Gower incognito

sparkling double century, I can't recall having another settled partner in any of my long innings.

That is astonishing and disturbing when you consider I have spent most of my time with England sandwiched between David Gower and Ian Botham. With players of their ability, I should have figured in more big partnerships with one or other of them than I have. Something seems to have gone wrong each time. It is astonishing also that David and Ian have not featured in many large partnerships together although they must have been in the same England side for around 100 innings.

Somebody has suggested that an extra element of competition creeps into partnerships when two star performers get together at the crease. Perhaps one or the other takes an extra risk bringing about his downfall when he is trying to look better than the chap at the other end. I obviously don't know what goes through the mind of David or Ian when they are together but I do know I happily give Ian the stage when I am batting with him. I have never tried to trade boundaries with him. If he is in that mood I'm quite content to push singles and give him the strike. If he can flay the bowling around, it makes it easier for me.

In my last six Test centuries by the end of 1984 I was left struggling to reach the three figure mark with tail end batsmen, wondering each time whether I would run out of partners before getting my ton. One of these days some unsuspecting opposition is going to pay heavily when two or three of us at the top of the order come off in the same innings.

Missing out on the 1983 World Cup Final at Lord's was a stunning blow. Within 12 months of first playing for England I was within one match of playing in the most important one day final in the game. Now I shall have to wait until India in 1987 and the next World Cup. However successfully organised, it will not be the same playing in a final over there as at Lord's.

We were really keyed up in 1983. The unit the selectors had given Bob Willis to lead looked exactly right, strong in batting and bowling, sound in the field and with a very good balance. We were playing so well by the quarter-final stage we strongly fancied our chances of making the final and even winning it even if it meant overcoming the West Indies at the last hurdle.

Our performances in the qualifying stage of the tournament had given us increased confidence after we had seen off New Zealand

27   Bob Willis posing inappropriately

with surprising comfort in the first game at the Oval when I managed to score a century.

We all thought Pakistan were going to be our most formidable opponents in our group, our opposition in the second match at Lord's. They fell more easily than New Zealand with us winning by eight wickets.

It was in that match that I saw probably the greatest spell of bowling Graham Dilley produced especially when he came back for four overs just after lunch. He did not take a wicket but he was lightning that afternoon coming in from the pavilion end. He shook up Pakistan and I can remember Imran Khan turning round to me after one express delivery from Dilley and saying 'What's going on, then?' He was clearly surprised by Dilley's pace that afternoon having played against him many times before.

We did stumble in our second match against New Zealand at Edgbaston when losing by two wickets with only one ball left but put that behind us when comfortably beating Pakistan a second time.

By winning our group we had avoided the West Indies in the semi-finals. Instead our opponents were India who had surprisingly qualified instead of Australia. The public could see nothing stopping us keeping the final date at Lord's but we were always worried about the match.

We knew that the Old Trafford wicket would suit the Indian attack with their collection of medium pacers better than it would suit ours which was based more on pace. The Indians had already proved that when beating the West Indies by 34 runs on the same ground in their first qualifying match.

To make sure of a place in the final we felt we needed to score at least 250, probably nearer 300. When we were bowled out for 213 by the likes of Kapil Dev, Roger Binny, Madan Lal and Mohinder Amarnath, we knew we were struggling. There was just not enough pace or bounce in the wicket to suit Willis, Dilley, Allott or Botham. It was more like a track the Indians are used to at home and they won with five overs and six wickets to spare.

I must admit I still did not fancy them for the final especially when they were bowled out for 183. The West Indies must have thought they had it won then and grew careless. They would probably have taken the trophy for a third time if they had been chasing 250 and forced to bat with more discretion.

Losing that semi-final was a great shock to the system.

CHAPTER 12

Conclusion

There was a great feeling of doom and gloom about the immediate future of English cricket at the end of the 1984 summer in England. That was understandable in a way. English cricket had suffered a blackwash against the West Indies which was followed immediately by the lame performance against Sri Lanka at Lord's. In addition Bob Willis, our one and only world class fast bowler, had announced his retirement after carrying the England attack, with occasional help from Ian Botham, for half a dozen series. Yet, I did not finish the summer as pessimistic about the rest of the 1980s as many other people.

I concede that the bowling strength is a worry although that might ease if Graham Dilley finds full fitness again after his neck trouble, Jonathan Agnew – who produced some deliveries as fast as those of Malcolm Marshall in his Test debut at the Oval – grows in strength and Norman Cowans continues to improve. They are all young, and their best years are ahead.

There is more encouragement on the spin bowling front too through the likes of Worcestershire's left arm spinner Richard Illingworth, plus the off spin of Yorkshire's Ian Swallow and Peter Such of Notts, all youngsters with a lot to learn but with obvious potential.

The future batting is in good order from what I saw around the county circuit in 1984 although, unfortunately, it was a pretty limited view with most of my time taken up with six Test matches and three one day internationals which prevented me playing in over half Northants' games.

The list is long of those who look as though they should be challenging for Test recognition in the not too distant future, early enough to keep me on my toes if I want to retain my place. I have already mentioned two in the Northants pair of Robin Boyd-Moss and Robert Bailey.

There are many others. Kent have three in Mark Benson, Derek Aslett and Laurie Potter and Essex have a couple in Chris Gladwin and Paul Prichard. The last two are quite a startling pair. Gladwin looks like a left handed version of Graham Gooch with the way he stands up and strikes the ball, while Prichard has the build and many of the mannerisms of his county captain, Keith Fletcher.

Lancashire's Neil Fairbrother must be high on the list and I know of one England selector who saw the little left hander for only 15 minutes at the crease and immediately remarked 'He's good enough for me.' Yorkshire have Ashley Metcalf, Notts have Paul Johnson and Leicestershire have John Whitaker while the Wells brothers of Sussex – Colin and Alan – must come into the reckoning soon.

By the very nature of their trade, the spinners I have mentioned may take a little longer to master their particular art before they reach a Test level but I shall be surprised if half a dozen of the other names do not manage a game for England before the end of the 1980s.

I said the list was long and encouraging. What English cricket has to ensure is that not one of the names I have mentioned – or any other player who may emerge – escapes the selectorial net and that they are all studied closely in every possible way. I have my own thoughts on that.

Let me say straight away even from my limited experience of English cricket that very little in the way of emerging talent appears to have escaped the selectors even though chairman Peter May along with his 1984 colleagues Alec Bedser, Phil Sharpe and Alan Smith, the Warwickshire secretary, all have full time jobs which keep them occupied.

Considering they have other employment – and some of their predecessors have been even more tied down – it is quite astonishing that players have been covered and vetted as well as they have been over the years.

Much of it is done by word of mouth, county secretaries, county managers, umpires and captains, passing on their views and judgements. Newspapers also help with cricket writers making claims on behalf of players they have caught on a good day. The averages help tell a story although, in my opinion, not a complete one. They do, however, act as a guide.

It is a system, for instance, which helped me into the England side so I have every reason to be grateful.

Yet I still wonder whether there might not be room for some changes to be made to assist the present four man selection committee in their task. To make sure that a professional sport, where the stakes are so high, the reputation and standing of the country at risk and even future sponsorship affected, is served in the most efficient way possible.

Take, for instance, the word of mouth system. I have witnessed more than one player who has looked sound in technique and application, a future Test player in the making, only to be puzzled when people in authority have dismissed that same person with the words 'so and so can't play.'

It all depends, of course, on who has seen what on a particular day and the conditions existing at the time. That brings me back to the one bouncer per over rule which existed. Under that rule most batsmen could look good against fast bowling in county cricket but a hopeless and lost cause when meeting three or four bouncers per over.

I know of other players from so called 'unfashionable' counties who complain that they never have a chance of catching a selectorial eye because they never see a selector on their home ground. That complaint may have been justified some years ago but I am sure it does not apply these days. Some players, of course, are unaware that a selector has been present and I see no reason why a selector should announce he is going here or there. He wants to see a player adopting his natural game rather than a pose just because somebody of importance may be around.

And just how accurate are the averages as a guide? They obviously give a fair indication at the end of a season which could help with the selection of a tour party. But they can be very misleading if taken as an indication of form after a month or even two months of a season just when the selectors are picking their sides for the Test series.

Averages do not and can not tell the full story of a batsman's capabilities as I know from my own case. After my first season with Northants in 1978 only a dozen or so other batsmen in the country finished with a better average in county cricket. It could be assumed from the figures that a certain A. J. Lamb was a pretty good all round player because the average covered the season as a whole during which I had been forced to cope with all kinds of conditions.

In fact, I struggled to come to terms with spin bowling in my first year. The surfaces in England offered more help to spin bowlers than the ones I had encountered in South Africa. And the county circuit contains some very wily and experienced wheeler dealers of spin, even if the bowlers concerned are not regarded as Test standard. Certainly, the majority were a better standard than I had encountered before in South Africa. It took me until half way through my second summer of county cricket before I was satisfied that my game enabled me to cope more than adequately.

An interesting case arose in 1984 concerning a youngish batsman – it would be unfair to mention his name – who was being pushed in some quarters for a place on the winter tour of India and Australia as a result of scoring six centuries during the summer. In bold black and white across one line in the list of averages, his figures appeared most encouraging. If he had been chosen for the tour, nobody could have argued against his selection – at least, based on his figures.

What they did not show, however, was the fact that he scored his six centuries against what were considered the six weakest county attacks and struggled when he came across a good one.

As I said earlier, I will not mention his name because scoring six centuries is an achievement. It also means that he undoubtedly did a very good job for his county side. The player concerned has every reason to be proud of his summer but his final average did not make him a Test player.

The mention of Test players brings me to another point. I often hear people complaining about a touring party make-up – even the selections made in a Test team towards the end of a summer – because individuals chosen do not appear in the top 20 in the batting and bowling averages published after every round of county matches. They do not for one very simple and basic reason. Their average over a season is reduced because they spend so much time playing in Test cricket against the very best in the world that their chances of picking up relatively easy runs or wickets in every day county cricket is considerably lessened.

For the future I would like to see the present four man selection committee given greater assistance by the addition of three others co-opted to make sure no player goes unnoticed, no stone unturned in the drive to make England the top Test playing country again.

I would suggest that England appoint a full-time manager, somebody else who has been retired from Test cricket for only a year or so plus two top first class umpires. They would all work with the present selection committee.

A manager surely makes sense in this modern age, somebody to look after the team at home and take some of the weight off the shoulders of the captain and who tours abroad with them every winter. It cannot be right that the selectors pick the tour party, never see them play overseas and then sit in judgement on those same players when they come to picking the next side at home.

It can be argued that the tour captain who helped in the selection of the tour party, is the selectorial representative on that tour. But there is no guarantee that the captain will be sitting down to help pick the first Test side at home the following summer. Keith Fletcher was not after he had led the England team to India in 1981/82. Bob Willis was not after leading England to New Zealand and Pakistan in 1984.

The Australian system I came across on my first tour there in 1982/83 compensated for this. The Australians made a short tour of Pakistan under the leadership of Kim Hughes in October and November 1982, returning home a week after we arrived there. As tour captain Kim Hughes sat on the selection committee picking the Australian side for the first Test against us – a committee which picked Greg Chappell as captain and asked Kim to stand down again.

It did not work out well for Kim. There seems little doubt the selectors had decided on asking Chappell to take over the captaincy again before that meeting took place. But at least they had Hughes with them so that they could hear first hand reports on how the players performed on the tour before making their decisions about the rest of the side.

Unfortunately I hardly knew Ken Barrington for he sounds the type of person I would have enjoyed. But he became almost an unofficial full-time manager until his tragic death on the last tour of the West Indies in 1980–81. He went on several tours in a row either as manager or assistant manager which must have been a considerable help to the selection committee of which he was a member. It gave the whole process a link through summer and winter. I know the lads appreciated it. They certainly appreciated having Ken around and the steady guidance he gave them.

Over the last three years Norman Gifford seems to have taken over the Ken Barrington role, acting as assistant manager on the last three tours although he is not a member of the selection panel. I can think of no better person to fill the role of a full-time manager in cricket.

He has been a selector so he knows what is required on that score. He has been a Test player. He has toured almost every cricket playing country in the world. And he knows the game inside out after all his years bowling left arm spin for Worcestershire and Warwickshire. He has always been a tremendous help to me.

If he were appointed I could see his job as the main co-ordinator working under the direct control of the chairman of selectors. He would organise the side and practice sessions during the actual playing of Test matches at home just as he has done overseas. He would also be on hand to help out the captain, perhaps offering words of advice, perhaps dealing with the media, acting as the link man between players and Press in helping to make sure there are no misunderstandings as have happened in recent years.

In between Test matches he could be visiting all the counties watching players, offering coaching tips, giving special advice, planning the advancement of young players and attending coaching clinics. Being full-time, he would have the opportunity to travel and always be available.

With the game changing so rapidly as it has done in recent years, the demands made on players vastly different from those of even 10 years ago, I think it would also be wise if the selectors could be assisted by somebody whose Test career has only recently come to an end.

That person would know the players and what makes them tick. He would know the countries and the differing requirements for touring India as opposed to those for visiting Australia or the West Indies. He would know the habits, the character of the players, their strengths and weaknesses having just lived and toured with them. An ideal role, say, for Bob Willis.

Although he has retired from playing Bob still has so much to offer England with his specialised knowledge. It would be a shame if that knowledge were not tapped immediately and I was delighted when he was appointed manager of the young England side in the Caribbean early in 1985. But the full England side still need his help now when every detail is still fresh in his mind. On past history it seems somebody has to be finished with Test cricket for a good many years before they are invited on to the selection panel by which time their specialised knowledge has been lost.

It is a very similar situation at county level. I believe far too many top class players are lost to the game upon retiring from first class cricket when they still have much to give cricket as a whole and their own county in particular. Far too few of them are asked to sit on committees once they have given up playing yet most would be willing to help out in some way or another. Cricket is a game which traps you for life. There are not many cricketers who leave the game unwilling to serve it in one capacity or another in an attempt to put something back for all the joy and pleasure the game has given them.

Now an umpire assisting the Test selection panel has always been a pet subject of mine for I know of no other individual who has such a close knowledge of what is actually going on.

An umpire sees a player in every type of condition whether he be a batsman or a bowler. He knows the batsmen who can survive on slow bounceless wickets and those who can cope with pace. He knows the batsmen who can look at home against spin bowling as against those who have relatively little idea how and when the ball is going to turn.

He knows the batsmen who shake and back away whenever a pace bowler starts marking out his long run and those who remain calm and collected. He knows the batsman who can stay in control of his feelings whatever is going on around him and those who can be easily distracted by sledging and backchat.

Above all he knows the batsmen who can cope with sheer pace, swing, seam and spin without being rattled. In other words, he knows an England player.

An umpire knows the bowlers, too. Those who can make things happen through their own ability rather than rely on help from the wicket. Those who are still trying at the end of the day when their captain asks them for one last effort on a flat nothing wicket and are not just going through the motions.

In England we are – rightly – proud of our umpires and the standard they maintain summer in and summer out. They are people picked for their coolness under pressure, experience, level headedness and ability to make sound and correct judgements.

An umpire helping on the Test selection panel would, in my view, add a fresh and interesting dimension that could only add to the quality of the work that goes on at present when the selectors sit down together.

When looking at the future of Test cricket from an England viewpoint, I also think we players have got to sit down and decide for ourselves just how much we are prepared to give when it comes to going on tour.

Now that there is a cricket tour every winter, the Test and County Cricket Board have done their best to accede to the wishes of the players in keeping those tours down to a bare minimum. I have been as strong as any other player in seeking that tours should be reduced to a three month period whenever possible. I have no wish to spend more than half a year away from my home which I do at present when taking away matches in the summer at home into consideration. It must be worse for those players with young families to support.

But, in trying to take care of the wishes of the players, there is also a danger of the Test and County Cricket Board cutting things a little too fine – for the best motives. As happened last winter when we ended up playing nothing else but Test matches and one day internationals for the last two months of our visit to New Zealand and Pakistan.

There was not sufficient time for us to get in the practice we needed to be fully prepared for the Test series when it started in New Zealand. Not sufficient time to get the right kind of practice in between Test matches or to be able to relax in between Tests in order that we could build ourselves up mentally and physically for the next big game.

The issue is even more difficult to settle these days because of the amount of one day internationals – the real money spinners in most countries – we are under pressure to play which directly affects the amount of first class games we play.

I am not blaming the Test and County Cricket Board. They have done their best to look after us. It is time, I believe, that we started to look at things ourselves.

We must be prepared to give up a little more time ourselves if we want to do the job properly. It is no use expecting a builder to erect a house in four weeks if he has said it is impossible to do the job in less than six weeks. Something is bound to go wrong with the house.

Results have not gone our way on recent tours abroad and I dislike being regarded as a failure when I return home to face my family, friends and neighbours. None of us do. I don't like it being broadcast to the world through newspapers, radio and television that England have failed again on tour. None of us do. We do have pride in ourselves and England.

If winning a Test series overseas means adding a couple of weeks to a tour in order that we should get the necessary preparation work in, the right kind of practice and the right time for relaxation, I am prepared to give those extra two weeks of my winter. And so must all the others who are selected to represent their country at a Test level.

Test matches are something special and we should be prepared to give more to make sure they stay that way. To be able to play in an international contest before a packed Lord's, Sydney, Lahore, Auckland, Jamaica and Calcutta is a great privilege, once experienced never to be forgotten. Playing alongside people – friend or foe – who become friends for life through the greatness of the game.

No matter what happens to me in the future, I shall always be grateful to England for giving me the opportunity to experience it all; to my parents Michael and Joan Lamb for having the good fortune to be born in England and, above all, to my wife Lindsay who gave up her own life and friends in South Africa to join me in Northampton where she has never stopped encouraging me in chasing my rainbow.

Index